KiSSING
IN THE KITCHEN

KiSSING
IN THE KITCHEN

COOKING *with* PASSION

Kevin T. Roberts

Food photography by
Christopher Marchetti

NORTHLAND
PUBLISHING

Text © 2007 by Kevin T. Roberts
Photography © Northland Publishing

www.northlandbooks.com

Composed in the Unites States of America
Printed in China

Edited by Claudine J. Randazzo
Designed by Sunny H. Yang
Food and Cover Photography by Christopher Marchetti

First Impression 2007
ISBN 10: 0-87358-931-9
ISBN 13: 978-0-87358-931-4

07   08   09   10   11   1   2   3   4   5

Roberts, Kevin T.
Kissing in the kitchen : cooking with passion / By Kevin T. Roberts.
p. cm.
Includes index.
ISBN-13: 978-0-87358-931-4 (pbk.)
ISBN-10: 0-87358-931-9 (pbk.)
1. Cookery. 2. Dating (Social customs) I. Title.
TX714.R587 2007
641.5--dc22
2007011390

The following recipes or versions of the following recipes were originally published by Kevin T. Roberts in *Munchies*:
Herb Roasted Red Potatoes
Roasted Garlic and Parmesan Cheese Guacamole

Publisher's Note: The recipes contained in this book are to be followed exactly as written. Neither the publisher nor the author is responsible for your specific health or allergy needs that may require medical supervision, or for any adverse reactions to the recipes contained in this book.

Contents

Introduction

GIVE ME A PLATE OF FOOD, a lovely conversation, a good bottle of wine, a beach or a fireplace, and I'm content. That's my idea of the ultimate date. Of course it didn't start out that way. I think at one time I would've been happy with a warm Budweiser and any warm body. Thankfully my tastes have changed a little, which basically means that I've become what I never thought I would…mature.

I've heard that we're supposed to live every day to the fullest, but our fast-food society—where there's no time to stop yet we always seem to be late—doesn't make it easy to live life to the fullest. We don't even have time to hold the door open for a woman anymore. Guess what? You'll never have a long-term, gratifying relationship with that attitude.

Breath…slow down…life is supposed to be like a good glass of wine. Drink it slowly, and make it last.

The most important thing before cooking for a date, or for anyone, is to ask, "What kind of food mood are you in?" and "What do you feel like drinking?" These two simple questions really show that you care about how your companion feels. So whether it's your first date and you have butterflies in your stomach, a special anniversary, or a chance to relight the fire (or you're just in trouble again) the recipes in this cookbook are sure to warm your companion's belly and, more importantly, heart.

You get three chances to make an impression when you've cooked a meal for your date: when you're prepping the meal, when you're cooking, and when you're eating. Once I almost burned down my apartment while cooking a meal for a lovely lady. You think she ever forgot that date? Of course not, especially when the fire department showed up, as well as the apartment manager who was not a happy camper. We had to go out to eat the next night, but I made an impression. I just recommend you make your impression by being creative and considerate and not by cooking with smoke, sirens, and crazed managers.

When you have a date it's all about focusing and really making it count. Call me fun, but I like rainy nights. What's better than a glass of wine, a shaggy 1970s bear rug, a little love, and a lot of food? Call me frisky, but I like hanging out with a potential lover while watching the sunset or sitting on the patio with a little conversation and a lot of food. Call me romantic because I like falling in love. And call me hungry because I love life and want to live it to the fullest with great food.

So…eat well, drink well, and live well!

To help you do that, read this book. Keep kissing in the kitchen and cooking with passion…and at least you'll have me until you find someone more worthy. You'll also have great dating tips and date meals to make along the way.

Plate, serve, and enjoy your food and company.

Kissing in the Pantry

LOOK THROUGH THE PANTRIES and refrigerators of people who cook, and certain must-have staples will be there. If your goal is to become a more organized cook—one who is prepared with the basic building blocks to try any new recipe—make sure your kitchen includes the items on this list.

Towels: Don't burn through paper towels. Get a collection of utilitarian towels that are not too big. I stuff a corner of my kitchen towel in my pocket while I'm cooking, or I keep it over my shoulder, so I like towels that are of a size and weight where that works. Don't tell anyone, but I take those white towels from hotel rooms and use those. When the towel is dirty, I throw it in the wash with my whites.

Extra Virgin Olive Oil: Always buy it in a dark bottle so it doesn't lose its valuable properties from light exposure. Keep it in a cupboard, not the refrigerator because it will coagulate.

Black Pepper Grinder: Fresh ground pepper from whole peppercorns adds a better flavor to foods.

Sea Salt: There's no need for iodized salt. Sea salt is more flavorful than iodized salt, and it won't melt in your hands while cooking.

Pesto Sauce: Great for all simple pastas.

Parmesan Cheese (grated): Keep some in the fridge and some in the freezer where it will last forever.

Romano Cheese (grated): Parmesan's cool cousin. It can be used interchangeably with Parmesan or combined with it. Keep some in the fridge and some in the freezer.

Frank's RedHot Sauce: It just won Best Sauce in America, and it's a great all around hot sauce.

Siricha Rooster Sauce: Great for any Asian cooking.

Whole Grain Mustard: Always use a quality mustard if you're making a sandwich or roasting a pork.

Vinegars: balsamic, rice, red wine	**Old Bay Seasoning**
Canned or frozen crabmeat	**Breadcrumbs**
All Purpose Flour	**Marsala Wine**
Maple Syrup	**Canola Oil**
Honey	**Ground Cinnamon**
Brown Rice	**Worcestershire Sauce**
Food Storage Containers	**Dried Herbs**
Nuts: almonds, walnuts, pine nuts	

Breakfast *in* Bed

COFFEE, TEA, OR ME? You can have all three—
you've earned it! Big yawn…another lazy weekend.
You try to sleep in, but you're so used to getting up in
the morning. This is a perfect time to get your coffee
or tea flowing, make breakfast for yourself and your
bedmate, and climb back in bed. There's nothing more
relaxing than being able to lie in bed and know you
have nothing to do and nowhere to go.

Start it off right. Breakfast is the most important meal of
the day because it kick-starts your metabolism. What
better way is there to enjoy burning calories than doing
nothing in bed? Here are some great recipes to get you
ready for a day of rolling around under the sheets.

WHAT'S HOT? • *Exotic fruit* • *Soy lattes* • *Morning sex*

The Frisky Frittata

It's already noon? Sounds like it's time for brunch. The perfect way to celebrate that Twilight-Zone time between breakfast and lunch is with a frittata. What makes these frittatas frisky is that they can be made several different ways. Here are 4 options, or get creative and make your own Frisky Frittata. I think I just like saying it: Frisky Frittata.

{
2 tablespoons extra virgin olive oil

6 eggs

2 tablespoons water

2 tablespoons milk

Salt and pepper to taste

OPTIONS FOR THE FRISKY FILLING:

Potato & Onion

2 red potatoes, chopped and boiled for 5 minutes to soften

1 medium yellow onion, chopped and sautéed for 3-5 minutes or until tender

Sausage & Cheese

1 cup sausage (your favorite kind), chopped and cooked

1 cup Cheddar cheese, shredded

Ham & Swiss Cheese

1 cup cooked ham, chopped

1 cup Swiss cheese, shredded

Veggie

An assortment of your favorite veggies (onion, bell pepper, mushroom, broccoli, spinach), chopped and sautéed for 3 minutes or until tender

1 cup Jack cheese, shredded

THE MOVES

1. Preheat oven to 375 degrees F.

2. Using the olive oil, grease a shallow baking dish.

3. In a mixing bowl whisk eggs, water, milk, salt, and pepper. Mix well until frothy.

4. Stir in the Frisky Fillings of your choice.

5. Pour into the baking dish and bake for 20-25 minutes or until a knife inserted in the center comes out clean.

Serves 2-4

Herb Roasted Red Potatoes

Potatoes are the number one veggie Americans eat. Unfortunately all we eat is the French fry version. Eating a potato any other way is good for you, and if you want to try something new, how about this super simple, healthy, and appetizing breakfast potato recipe?

4–8 red potatoes, washed and quartered

1/4 cup olive oil (extra virgin is the least acidic)

1 tablespoon herb mix (see 4-1-1 Tips)

THE MOVES

1. Preheat oven to 375 degrees F.

2. In a large mixing bowl add potatoes, olive oil, and herbs. Stir well to coat.

3. Place potato mixture in a shallow baking dish and cover.

4. Bake for 20-30 minutes or until potatoes are fork tender and a little crispy.

Serves 2

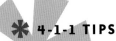

4-1-1 TIPS

* Russet potatoes are used more for baked potatoes because they are so soft, so I recommend using any other type of potato besides Russet for this recipe.

* The herb mix can be whatever fresh herbs you have or any pre-mixed blend of dry Italian herbs. Lawry's makes a good herb mix.

* For less clean-up, place the potato mixture in tin foil, wrap securely, and place the tin foil pouch directly on the oven rack to bake.

Flirty French Toast

If this recipe doesn't get you "in the mood," nothing will. Here's my twist. I like to use fresh French bread cut into thick slices, or find another fresh bread you like, such as Italian or a round loaf.

> **1 tablespoon butter**
>
> **4 eggs**
>
> **1 cup milk**
>
> **1 teaspoon cinnamon**
>
> **A pinch of nutmeg**
>
> **1 loaf fresh French bread cut into 1-2 inch slices**
>
> **Maple syrup**

THE MOVES

1. Heat a large skillet over medium heat.
2. In a shallow bowl whisk the eggs, milk, cinnamon, and nutmeg together.
3. Add the butter to the skillet and melt.
4. Dip bread slices in the egg mixture, coating both sides well.
5. Place the bread in the skillet and cook until golden brown on each side.
6. Serve immediately with butter and maple syrup.

Serves 2-4

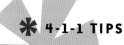

❋ 4-1-1 TIPS

* Serve with fresh fruit, such as sliced strawberries, blueberries, blackberries, kiwis, or mangoes.
* Instead of maple syrup, use jam.
* Try using Hawaiian sweet bread.

Breakfast Tacos

This recipe is a nice change from just having the same eggs again and again and again. Breakfast tacos are a refreshing and easy way to mix up those monotonous breakfasts.

- 1 teaspoon olive oil
- 4 eggs
- 4 flour tortillas, taco-size
- 1 16-ounce can refried beans
- 1/2 cup Parmesan cheese
- 4 tablespoons hot sauce

THE MOVES

1. Heat a large skillet or pan over medium heat. Add olive oil.

2. In a mixing bowl whisk eggs until blended.

3. Add eggs to the skillet and cook until desired doneness. (See 4-1-1 Tips for scrambling eggs.)

4. Put beans in a bowl and cover with a paper towel so beans don't get all over the inside of your microwave. Nuke for about 1 minute or until beans are nice and warm.

5. Heat the tortillas over the open burner, flipping often so they don't burn.

6. Assemble the tacos by first spreading the beans on the tortilla, then the eggs, then the cheese, and then the hot sauce.

Serves 2

✳ 4-1-1 TIPS

* Mission tortillas are abundant in stores, and another great twist for this recipe is to try Mission's flavored tortillas such as whole wheat, sun-dried tomato, and pesto.

* A tip when scrambling eggs is to swirl them in a circular motion while cooking.

* Parmesan cheese is the cleanest and healthiest cheese to eat. You can change the tacos by using other cheeses if you like.

White Omelet

Using only the egg whites is a healthy way to still have eggs and benefit from the protein but eliminate the cholesterol that is in the yoke. Cream cheese and eggs go great together, too. The cream cheese melts in the omelets and creates a warm and creamy filling. Just like the cover of the Beatles' White album, everything is white. But in our colorful and eclectic world, it's OK to add some color. Chopped tomatoes work well with this white canvas of food.

2-3 teaspoons butter or oil

4-8 egg whites

2 tablespoons milk (this makes the eggs fluffy)

4-6 tablespoons soft Philadelphia cream cheese

THE MOVES

1. In a medium skillet warm butter or oil over medium heat, spreading evenly over the skillet.

2. Whisk egg whites and milk together.

3. Add half of the egg mixture to the skillet, spreading evenly around the skillet so the omelet is equal in thickness and width.

4. When the egg is cooked about halfway, lift the edges carefully with a spatula until it releases from the skillet but is still intact. Flip the omelet over and cook on the other side.

5. Add half of the cream cheese (and other fillings, if using) on half of the omelet. Fold the omelet over so it looks like a half-moon, and cook until cream cheese is melted.

6. Repeat with the remaining egg mixture and cream cheese.

Serves 2-4

✳ 4-1-1 TIP

As a substitute for the cream cheese, these combinations also work well: chèvre (goat cheese) and sun-dried tomatoes, mushrooms and Jack cheese, steak and Gorgonzola cheese.

Ham and Biscuits *with* Red Eye Gravy

It's another one of those mornings from a late night of partying and hanging out. As you roll around in bed and think about what a great time you had, you start to crave your daily coffee and greasy meat. Wipe the sleep from your eyes and make this eye-opening breakfast.

{
Virginia cured ham, sliced thin

1 cup coffee

Pillsbury biscuits, baked according to package

THE MOVES

1. Put biscuits in the oven and bake according to directions. When done, cut biscuits in half.

2. In a large frying pan fry the ham slices over medium high heat until nice and brown on both sides. Remove the ham, but leave the grease in the pan.

3. Add the cup of coffee to the pan, stir well, and let reduce until the liquid becomes the consistency of gravy.

4. Place a piece of ham on top of each biscuit half and pour red eye gravy over each one.

Serves 2-4

* 4-1-1 TIPS

* You can add butter or a little oil to the pan, but the natural oil from the ham will come out when heated. If you use butter, use the spreadable kind that contains canola oil (Land O Lakes spreadable butter is really good).

* For a really tasty ham, order from www.smithfieldcollection.com.

* Scrambled or fried eggs also go well with this breakfast.

Old School Potatoes Au Gratin

After another long week of indentured servitude, it's fun to revert back to the old days and pretend you're a kid again when life was so much simpler. This recipe is sure to make you feel nostalgic and remember the good ol' days.

- 1/2 stick butter
- 1/4 cup flour
- 1 teaspoon salt
- 1 teaspoon mustard
- 2 cups milk
- 1 8-ounce package Kraft shredded Cheddar cheese
- 1/2 cup Parmesan cheese
- 1 small onion, chopped
- 6 medium-size Russet/Idaho potatoes, washed, peeled, and sliced

THE MOVES

1. Preheat the oven to 350 degrees F.
2. Melt butter over medium heat in a medium saucepan.
3. Mix flour, salt, and mustard in the pan.
4. Gradually add milk, stirring constantly until thickened.
5. Add both cheeses and onion, and stir until cheese is melted.
6. Grease a baking dish with vegetable spray or butter.
7. Layer sliced potatoes and cheese sauce alternating and ending with potatoes on top.
8. Bake at 350 degrees F for 1 hour or until potatoes are nice and tender.

Serves 2-4

4-1-1 TIP

For a more crunchy bite, top with breadcrumbs. "Au Gratin" means sprinkled with breadcrumbs, mixed with cheese, and browned before serving.

Get Up and Go Protein Smoothie

Here's a fun, creative, and very tasty smoothie. If you want to make up your own recipes, just start with your favorite juice, then add nuts for protein or use protein powder, fresh fruits for fiber, and whatever else you want to throw in the blender. I recommend everything but the kitchen sink.

1 cup ice

I cup juice (orange, tangerine, pineapple; milk or soy milk can be substituted for juice)

1/2 cup blueberries (or anything ending in "berry")

1 banana

1/2 cup almonds (or 2 tablespoons protein powder)

1 tablespoon honey

THE MOVES

1. Combine ice, juice, blueberries, banana, almonds, and honey in a blender.

2. Blend well for a few minutes or until all ingredients are thoroughly mixed.

3. Pour into two tall glasses.

Serves 2

APHRODISIAC

Many cultures regard certain foods as erotic stimulants because of their phallic resemblance. Researchers have discovered that some of the most well known edible aphrodisiacs do in fact contain vitamins and minerals that contribute specifically to a healthy libido. There's nothing sexier than a romantic dinner to get you in the mood for love. Try using these foods in your cooking to kick-start your love life.

APHRODISIAC #1: Carrots

Believed to be a stimulant for us males. The phallus shaped carrot has been associated with stimulation since ancient times. High in beta-carotene.

APHRODISIAC #2: Bananas

The banana flower has a marvelous phallic shape and is partially responsible for the popularity of the banana as an aphrodisiac food. A long-held myth is that Adam and Eve started covering their "nudity" with banana leaves rather than fig leaves. From a more practical standpoint, bananas are rich in potassium and B vitamins, necessities for sex hormone production.

Fried-egg Sandwich *with* Bacon and Mustard Greens

My nana loves this dish and makes it for me on the weekends. And NO, I don't live with my nana…anymore. She makes it for me when I go to visit her.

{ Cooking spray

4 eggs

4 slices bacon

1 bunch mustard greens, cleaned, dried, and tough skins removed

Sauce of your choosing (see Sauce Options)

4 slices of your favorite bread

Sauce Options:

- Mix equal amounts of mayonnaise, pickle relish, and catsup.

- Mix equal amounts of Frank's RedHot Sauce and catsup.

- Mix equal amounts of Italian dressing and Parmesan cheese.

THE MOVES

1. In a medium skillet coated with cooking spray fry eggs on medium heat until desired doneness. Remove and keep warm.

2. In the same pan cook the bacon. Transfer cooked bacon from the pan to a paper towel.

3. Discard all but a couple of tablespoons of the bacon grease, leaving just enough in the pan to quickly sauté the mustard greens.

4. Cut the mustard greens into 5-inch-long pieces. Cook in the bacon grease until just wilted.

5. Toast all of the bread and spread sauce evenly on two pieces, then place two eggs each on the pieces of toast with sauce.

6. Place the bacon on top of the eggs, then distribute the mustard greens evenly, and top with the remaining pieces of toast.

Serves 2

4-1-1 TIPS

* This recipe also works well with scrambled eggs or egg whites.
* Canadian bacon is also very tasty and can be substituted for the bacon.
* Rye bread works well with this sammie, or you can go with Nana's love, white bread. And no, she doesn't live in a trailer.

Hearty Hash & Eggs

You can use just about any potato you like for this recipe. The trick is to rinse the excess starch from the potatoes after you grate them. I like to put my eggs right on the hash, so when I break the yoke, all the warm yellow lava of love slowly melts into the taters.

{
- 2 tablespoons olive oil or vegetable oil
- 1 medium onion, chopped
- 1 green bell pepper, chopped
- 2 garlic cloves, minced
- 2 slices of ham, diced
- 2-4 potatoes
- Salt and pepper to taste
- 2-4 eggs, cooked to your liking

THE MOVES

1. Preheat oven to 450 degrees F.

2. Wash, peel, and grate potatoes. Place grated potatoes in a colander and rinse in cold water. Set aside.

3. In a large ovenproof skillet add oil and heat over medium heat.

4. Add the onion, green pepper, garlic, and ham. Sauté for about 2 minutes.

5. Add potatoes and sauté for another 3-4 minutes. Take the skillet and place in the oven. Bake for 15-20 minutes or until potatoes are nice and crunchy.

6. Cook eggs about 5 minutes before the hash is done. (This is where it's good to have a clock or a watch or a sundial. Cooking, like on *Iron Chef*, is all about timing, but you're no Iron Chef, so no need to be stressed. Just remember that the goal is to have the hash warm and the eggs done at the same time.)

7. When the hash and eggs are done, spoon hash onto the center of two plates and then place the eggs on top of the hash.

Serves 2

 4-1-1 TIPS

* Add some Parmesan cheese after you plate the food to give it a nice cheesy kick.

* If you like catsup with your hash, try making a spicy version by mixing equal amounts of catsup and hot sauce.

* Don't worry about garlic breath. If you both eat it then the bad breath gets cancelled out because you both taste and smell like it.

Crustless Quiche

It's seven o'clock in the morning. It's the weekend. No one wants to make a crust—most of us don't even know how to make a crust. So try this easy egg dish to start your day.

{
1 cup eggs (4 eggs) or any cholesterol-free egg product

1/2 cup cooked meat (sausage, ham, chicken, or turkey)

3 tablespoons veggies (use your favorite chopped-up veggies)

1 cup shredded cheese (use your favorite)

1 1/2 cups milk

Salt and pepper to taste

THE MOVES

1. Preheat oven to 350 degrees F.

2. Grease a 9-inch pie pan with olive oil or a nonstick cooking spray.

3. In a large bowl combine the eggs, meat, veggies, cheese, milk, and salt and pepper. Mix well.

4. Pour the mixture into the greased pie pan.

5. Bake at 350 degrees F for 15 minutes until center is cooked through and it has a nice golden brown color.

Serves 2

 4-1-1 TIPS

* White cheese is less greasy than Cheddar and Colby cheese.

* Mixed fresh veggies can be: onion, green peppers, tomatoes, potatoes.

* The quiche is fully cooked when an inserted knife comes out clean.

Chipotle Mexican Eggs

You're craving a spicy twist this morning. Try this south-of-the-border inspiration. Chipotles are smoked jalapeños and they come canned in an adobo sauce, which when used together create a robust and smoky flavor. This is a common combination found in the Southwest and Mexico.

{
1 teaspoon oil

1 small onion, chopped

1 7-ounce can chipotle chiles in adobo sauce, finely chopped

1 16-ounce can of diced tomatoes

4 tortillas

4 eggs

1/2 cup Mexican 4-blend cheese

THE MOVES

1. In a medium skillet over high heat add the oil, onion, chipotles, and tomatoes. Bring it to a boil and then set to simmer.

2. In another skillet fry the eggs to your liking.

3. Heat the tortillas over a burner until crispy. Set the tortillas aside.

4. Lay eggs over tortillas and then pour sauce over eggs.

Serves 2

✳ 4-1-1 TIPS

* Either flour or corn tortillas may be used.

* Fresh tomatoes work great in this recipe, but if you're feeling lazy, S&W has canned ready cut tomatoes (also known as petite cut).

* Instead of heating the tortillas directly on the burner, they can be fried in a skillet with a little bit of oil.

* Over-easy and over-medium eggs work best as the warm yolk blends beautifully with the sauce.

Nibbles

A LITTLE NIBBLE HERE.
A big nibble there. Appetizers,
tapas, hors d'oeurves—or
whatever you want to call these
tasty morsels, what's great about
Nibbles is that they won't weigh
you down and make you feel
stuffed and tired. So keep eating,
talking, and flirting because
Nibbles are just small and simple
plates with big flavor. Make 3 or
4 of these different and delicious
plates and have fun.

WHAT'S HOT? • *Spanish wines and cheeses*
• *Extra virgin olive oil, soybean oil, and sunflower oil* • *Sharing*

Sleep-over Spinach

The first time I made this dish, I created a mouthful of heaven, and a "friend with benefits" that wouldn't leave. The creaminess of the Brie with the warm spinach melts in your mouth.

{
1/2 cup water

1 bunch fresh spinach, washed and stems removed

4 slices (about 4 ounces) Brie cheese, rind removed

THE MOVES

1. Bring the water to a boil in a medium saucepan.

2. Add spinach and boil for about 2 minutes, stirring.

3. Drain spinach in a colander, squeeze, and then return to warm saucepan.

4. Add cheese, stirring and blending.

5. Place in a shallow bowl because there will be some liquid, and you don't want it running off the plate. Add some pine nuts for a crunchy bite.

Serves 2

Manchego Cheese *with* Olive Tapenade

Manchego cheese is delicious and has a slight piquant and nutty flavor. Made from sheep's milk, it's the most popular cheese in Spain.

{
1 pound manchengo cheese

1 8-ounce jar olive tapenade

2 tablespoons minced fresh parsley

THE MOVES

1. Cut cheese into 1-inch-thick triangles.

2. Spread 1 teaspoon of olive tapenade on each cheese slice.

3. Sprinkle with a pinch of parsley.

4. Arrange pieces on a platter in a creative way.

Serves 2-4

Insalata Caprese

This simple and delicious Italian salad means "salad in the style of Capri," and it calls for fresh mozzarella. The colors also represent those of the Italian flag.

2 large tomatoes

1 pound fresh mozzarella

1 bunch fresh basil, rinsed and dried

2-3 tablespoons extra virgin olive oil

Salt and pepper to taste

THE MOVES

1. Slice the tomatoes into 1/2-inch-thick rounds.

2. Slice the mozzarella into 1/4-inch-thick rounds.

3. Cut the basil into thin strips.

4. Arrange alternating slices of tomato and mozzarella on a platter.

5. Sprinkle cut basil leaves on top of the tomatoes and cheese.

6. Drizzle with olive oil and then sprinkle with salt and pepper.

Serves 2-4

✳ 4-1-1 TIPS

* Fresh, or wet, mozzarella is available now at most stores. It comes packaged in water. When you get it home, it's wise to take it out of the water it came in and put it in a container and add fresh water to it.

* The best tomatoes to use for this dish are heirloom and Roma (also called "plum").

* The photos on the right show a trick to cutting basil really thin and long.

Pan Fried Goat Cheese *with* Juicy Marinara Sauce

Making marinara sauce is quite easy. But if you're feeling lazy you can use any marinara sauce. I recommend Newman's Own because it's organic, Newman gives to charity, and he's just cool.

{
1 5.5-ounce roll goat cheese (use an 11-ounce log to double the recipe)

Simple Marinara Sauce (see below), or 1 jar of your favorite sauce

1 loaf French bread, cut into 1/2-inch slices

THE MOVES

1. Slice goat cheese into 1-inch-thick rounds.

2. Warm marinara sauce on the stovetop or microwave. When the sauce is warm, spread it on large plate or platter.

3. Preheat nonstick skillet over medium heat.

4. Fry cheese pieces in skillet for about 1 minute on each side.

5. Place fried goat cheese slices uniformly on top of marinara sauce.

6. Toast bread slices and arrange around the marinara/cheese platter.

7. Spread marinara and goat cheese on bread and enjoy.

Serves 2

Simple Marinara Sauce

{
2 tablespoons olive oil

1 28-ounce can whole, peeled, tomatoes

4 cloves garlic, minced

1 tablespoon Lawry's Pinch of Herbs or any herb mix

Salt and pepper to taste

THE MOVES

1. Heat the oil in a medium saucepan over high heat.

2. Coarsely chop tomatoes.

3. Sauté garlic in the oil for about 1 minute. Add tomatoes, herb mix, salt, and pepper. Bring to a boil. Reduce heat and simmer for about 20 minutes or until nice and thick.

Serves 2-4

Hot Dates

How cool is it to eat hot dates while you're on a hot date? When you cook the date it caramelizes with the cheese and bacon creating this unbelievable velvety sensation. I had these for the first time at Fuego in Atlanta, but they are made and eaten throughout Spain.

10 dates

1 4-ounce container crumbled Gorgonzola cheese (or blue cheese)

10 bacon slices

10 toothpicks

THE MOVES

1. Remove the pits from the dates.

2. Stuff each date with a teaspoonful of cheese. (Using your fingers works best.) Close date after stuffing.

3. Wrap a slice of bacon around the date and secure it with a toothpick to keep the bacon from unraveling when cooking.

4. Grill for about 5 minutes on each side or until bacon is cooked and crispy. Remove toothpick or skewer and serve.

Serves 2

Lumpia

This Philippine "love stick" is like a meat-style egg roll. My Irish buddy had these at his girlfriend's house and hasn't left since. Now they're engaged; thank you, Lumpia Gods!

{
1 pound ground turkey

1 small onion, minced

1 large carrot, minced

1 celery stalk, minced

1 green onion, minced

Salt and pepper to taste

1 egg white

1 package egg roll wrappers

1/2 cup vegetable oil

THE MOVES

1. In a large mixing bow mix ground meat, onion, carrot, celery, green onion, salt, and pepper.

2. In a small mixing bowl whisk the egg white.

3. Place a spoonful of the meat mixture (about the length of a finger) onto the edge of each egg roll wrapper. Fold in the outer edges of the wrapper to partly cover the meat mixture and roll it up lengthwise. Use egg white as a glue to seal the lumpia closed while rolling.

4. Add oil to a large skillet and heat on medium high. Cook lumpia, turning, until golden brown.

5. Serve with Kikkoman Sweet 'n Sour Sauce, spicy mustard, or a plum sauce.

Serves 8-10

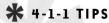

✳ 4-1-1 TIPS

* Ground beef can be substituted for the turkey, but it's a lot more greasy.

* Egg roll wrappers are available at any Asian market or in the deli section of your local grocery store.

* The lumpia can also be deep fried. I use a Rival deep fryer.

Sautéed Mushroom, Blue Cheese, and Pecan Relish *with* Toast Points

This delightful dish is eaten with toast points. Make sure to buy mushrooms that are intact and firm.

2 tablespoons olive oil

1 8-ounce container Crimini mushrooms, cleaned with a paper towel, stems removed

1/2 cup chopped pecans

1/2 cup crumbled blue cheese

1 tablespoon balsamic vinegar

10 slices of good-quality bread, sliced

THE MOVES

1. Thinly slice mushrooms.

2. In a large skillet heat oil over medium heat. Add the mushrooms and pecans. Sauté for about 5-7 minutes or until mushrooms are nice and tender.

3. Add the blue cheese and balsamic vinegar. Toss and coat all ingredients well. Remove from heat and set aside.

4. Remove crust from bread. Cut slices in half diagonally to form 4 triangles.

5. Preheat oven to 400 degrees F.

6. Arrange a single layer of bread pieces on a baking sheet and bake for 4-5 minutes, or until nice and toasted.

7. Serve with a spoonful of the relish on top of each toast point.

Serves 5

✳ 4-1-1 TIPS

* French bread works well for making the toast points.

* Crimini mushrooms are also known as Italian browns.

* Avoid mushrooms that are wrinkled, slimy, or spotted (you know, kind of like your ex).

Baked Sweet Potato Fries

I don't know why, but when I think of this recipe it seems complicated. In reality, it can't be any simpler—especially if you own a deep fryer. These are very tasty baked in the oven or cooked on a grill.

2 sweet potatoes, peeled

2-3 tablespoons vegetable oil

Sea salt and pepper to taste

THE MOVES

1. Preheat oven to 350 degrees F or fire up that barbecue.

2. Cut sweet potatoes lengthwise into long, uniform pieces.

3. In a medium mixing bowl stir together sweet potatoes, oil, salt, and pepper until the potatoes are well coated.

4. Arrange a single layer of the sweet potatoes in a shallow baking dish.

5. Bake 20-30 minutes or until nice and crispy.

Serves 2

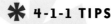 **4-1-1 TIPS**

* The cool new oils to use are soybean or sunflower oil. But vegetable and olive oil work fine, too.

* This recipe also makes a great side dish to meat and chicken entrees.

* Instead of plain catsup, try my Cayenne Catsup Sauce, which is equal parts catsup and Frank's RedHot Sauce.

Stuffed Mushrooms

If your date likes mushrooms, then these mushrooms stuffed with all this love will be a hit. These aren't magic mushrooms, unless you add a little of your good sense of humor when you serve them.

10 medium mushrooms

1 cup Santa Barbara Bay Cajun Krab Blend

1/2 stick butter, melted

3 tablespoons breadcrumbs

3 tablespoons Parmesan cheese

THE MOVES

1. Preheat oven to 450 degrees F.

2. Clean the mushrooms with a paper towel and remove the stems.

3. In a large bowl mix the Krab Blend, melted butter, breadcrumbs, and Parmesan cheese.

4. Stuff each mushroom with the mixture making a nice little molded mound.

5. Bake for 7 minutes or until mushrooms are soft and stuffing is golden brown.

6. Arrange in a circular pattern on a serving platter.

Serves 5

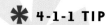

✳ 4-1-1 TIP

Saltine cracker crumbs can be substituted for breadcrumbs.

Avocado Spread

Avocados are velvety and have a nutty flavor. This recipe is a fresh and creamy alternative to making guacamole. In Chile, they call this recipe mantequilla de los pobres, which means "Poor People's Butter."

2 Hass avocados

Juice of 2 limes

1/3 cup olive oil

2 tablespoons Parmesan cheese

Salt and pepper to taste

Crackers

THE MOVES

1. Scoop out the flesh of the avocado and put it in a blender or Cuisinart with the lime juice, olive oil, Parmesan cheese, salt, and pepper.

2. Blend until mixture is smooth and spreadable (about one minute).

3. Place spread in a bowl and arrange crackers on a platter around the bowl.

Serves 2

 4-1-1 TIPS

* Avocados are high in a good fat called monounsaturated fat. They are also high in vitamin E, which is good for your skin and nails—but don't tell that to your guy friends.

* Hass avocados are now available year-round.

* Add a dash of your favorite hot sauce for a little extra bite.

* A sliced baguette can be substituted for the crackers.

Hot Days, Cool Salads

Chilly Nights, Warm Soups

Hot Days, Cool Salads

NOTHING IS MORE ROMANTIC than a warm summer evening when the burnt orange sun is setting slowly over the horizon, creating a peaceful and contented feeling within you. You've survived another hellishly hot day, and now you're finally feeling a little hungry. Of course, the last thing you want to do is put on some clothes, turn on the oven, and cook something. That would put the air conditioner on strike, and you can't have that.

These salad recipes are light and refreshing—just the way the ultimate summer date should be. But I definitely recommend putting some clothes on before your date comes over.

WHAT'S HOT? • *Toasted nuts* • *Goat cheese* • *Wild field greens*

Blue Cheese and Walnut Salad

Blue Cheese has such a pleasant yet bold, smooth bite, and walnuts give it that salty crunch.

- 1 small red onion
- 1 package European mixed greens
- 1 package Planters chopped walnuts
- 2 ounces crumbled blue cheese
- 1/4 cup raspberry vinaigrette dressing

THE MOVES

1. Slice the red onion into thin strips.
2. In a large bowl combine the greens, walnuts, red onion, and blue cheese.
3. Add the dressing, mix well, kick up your feet, and eat.

Serves 2-4

4-1-1 TIP

Look in the Sexy Sauces chapter, for my homemade mustard vinaigrette that can be substituted for the raspberry vinaigrette.

Arugula Salad *with* Granny Smith Apples

The tangy, crunchy bite of the apple slices gives this salad a unique flavor, especially if you add Gorgonzola or goat cheese.

{
1 Granny Smith apple

1 bag arugula salad mix

4 tablespoons crumbled Gorgonzola or goat cheese

4 ounces of your favorite vinaigrette dressing (Gorgonzola vinaigrette or balsamic vinaigrette)

THE MOVES

1. Thinly slice the apple. Grill the slices until they are warm and have grill marks, about 3 minutes each side. Set aside.

2. Rinse and dry the arugula.

3. In a medium serving bowl, combine salad mix, apple slices, cheese, and vinaigrette. Toss well and serve.

Serves 2

Roasted Beet and Garlic Salad
with Goat Cheese

Roasting beets is super simple but also super impressive. When beets are roasted they change their flavor and complexity. Golden beets are delicious too.

{
2 beets, red or gold

3 tablespoons extra virgin olive oil

8 cloves garlic, peeled and left whole

Salt and pepper to taste

1/2 cup crumbled goat cheese

THE MOVES

1. Preheat oven to 375 degrees F.

2. Peel and quarter the beets.

3. In a medium bowl combine the beets, olive oil, garlic, salt, and pepper.

4. Transfer to a baking dish and roast in the oven for 30 minutes or until fork tender.

5. Remove from the oven and let cool.

6. Add the goat cheese, stirring until mixed thoroughly.

Serves 2

4-1-1 TIP

If you can find baby beets, use those and roast them whole with the skin on. The skin will slip off easily when cooked.

APHRODISIAC #3: Garlic

The heat in garlic is said to stir sexual desires. Make sure you and your date both eat garlic because then the bad breath associated with garlicky meals is canceled out because you both have it. Garlic has been used for centuries to cure everything from the common cold to the broken heart.

APHRODISIAC #4: Arugula

An aromatic salad green, it has been documented as an aphrodisiac since the first century. Arugula greens are frequently used in salads and pasta.

APHRODISIAC #5: Avocado

The Aztecs called the avocado tree "Ahuacuatl," which translated means "testicle tree." This is a delicious fruit with a sensuous texture. Avocados also are high in a good fat that benefits the skin and complexion.

APHRODISIAC #6: Pine Nuts

Zinc is a key mineral necessary to maintain male potency, and pine nuts are rich in zinc.

APHRODISIAC #7: Fig

An open fig is thought to emulate the female sex organs. When a man breaks open a fig and eats it in front of his lover, it is a very potent and erotic act.

Endive Salad *with* Honey Vinaigrette

Endive is the yellow-whitish, purplish alien-looking lettuce pod at the store. As Nana says, "They're chock full of vitamins." They're also chock full of flavor.

{
2 heads large endive

1 Fuji apple

2 tablespoons crumbled blue cheese

1/2 cup toasted pecans

2 tablespoons honey

2 tablespoons white wine vinegar

1 tablespoon olive oil

THE MOVES

1. Trim the ends of the endive and then cut lengthwise into thin slivers.

2. Core the apple and thinly slice.

3. In bowl combine endive, apple, blue cheese, and pecans.

4. In a separate bowl mix honey, vinegar, and olive oil.

5. Pour the oil mixture over endive salad and blend well.

Serves 2

4-1-1 TIP

If you cannot find toasted pecans or would like to toast them yourself, just put them on some tin foil and bake at 350 degrees F in the oven. Or you can get fancy-schmancy and toast them in a pan over an open flame. Just make sure if you do it this way that someone's watching!

Corn, Mango, and Jicama Salad

Jicama, pronounced HEE-kah-mah, is the hot new root vegetable used in a lot of tapas-style restaurants. It is a large, beet-shaped Mexican root with thin brown skin and crisp white flesh. You can eat it raw or cooked. The taste is something between an apple and a pear but not as sweet.

{
2-4 ears corn

2 mangoes

1 jicama

1 small red onion

1 tablespoon chopped cilantro

Juice of 1 lime

Salt and pepper to taste

THE MOVES

1. Cook the corn in a pot of boiling water.

2. Drain and cool the corn.

3. Peel the mangoes, remove the pit, and dice.

4. Peel the jicama and dice.

5. Dice the onion.

6. Cut the kernels off of the corn.

7. In a medium bowl combine the corn kernels, mango, jicama, onion, cilantro, lime juice, salt, and pepper. Toss well.

8. Keep cool in the fridge until ready to serve.

Serves 2-4

Chilly Nights, Hot Soups

WHEN IT'S FIVE O' CLOCK and you're driving home from work and its already dark and spooky out, this is the time of year to slap on the pajamas a bit early and grab a blanket. I like to call it Cuddle Time! There's nothing wrong with a little cuddling; don't save it just for Sleepy Time! Once you've cuddled and gotten the exterior warmed up, it's time to get the soul warmed up.

WHAT'S HOT? • *Playing old-school board games* • *Sitting by the fireplace* • *Cuddling under thick blankets*

Lemongrass Soup

This soup is called Tom Yum in Thailand. I had to figure out this recipe on my own. There's a Thai restaurant down the street from my house that makes this soup so well—that taste of lemongrass is so fresh and distinguishable.

{
6 stalks lemongrass
1/2 bunch cilantro, washed
6 cups chicken broth
1 cup quartered button mushrooms
Juice of 1 lime

THE MOVES

1. Remove the outer layer of the lemongrass, then cut and split the bulbs.
2. Coarsely chop the cilantro.
3. In a medium soup pot over medium heat bring chicken broth to a simmer.
4. Add the lemongrass and simmer for 5 minutes.
5. Add the cilantro, mushrooms, and lime juice and cook for another 5 minutes.

Serves 2-4

French Onion Soup

I had about 4 bowls of this when I was staying with friends in Boston. You know how cold it gets in Boston? It was so cold, I didn't want to get out of the car coming from the airport. Once inside, we made this wonderfully light yet fulfilling soup. The trick is to use Fresh mozzarella cheese.

{
- **2 cloves garlic**
- **3 onions (1 red, 1 white, 1 yellow)**
- **1/4 stick butter (2 tablespoons)**
- **1 tablespoon flour**
- **1 tablespoon Parmesan cheese**
- **4 15-ounce cans beef broth**
- **2 thick slices fresh mozzarella**

THE MOVES

1. Peel and mince garlic cloves.

2. Slice onions into rings.

3. In a medium soup pot add butter and melt over medium high heat. Add garlic and sauté for about 2 minutes.

4. Add onions and sauté until tender, stirring occasionally.

5. Stir in flour and Parmesan cheese.

6. Pour beef broth into pot, turn down the heat, and let simmer for 30 minutes.

7. Place one slice each of mozzarella in the bottom of soup bowls and pour soup into the bowls.

Serves 4

 4-1-1 TIPS

* Add a slice of French bread to the bottom of the bowl, and then place the mozzarella cheese on top of bread before pouring the soup in.

* Herbed mozzarella works well, too.

Classic Minestrone *with* Sage & Rustic Bread

As soon as the sun starts going down and a chill is in the air, I think to myself, what warm food am I going to eat tonight for dinner? Then I remember; it's all about the soup. Here's my rendition of this classic Italian soup that is sure to keep you warm for nights to come.

{
- **3 tablespoons olive oil**
- **3-5 cloves garlic, peeled**
- **1 medium onion**
- **2 carrots**
- **1 small zucchini**
- **5 Roma tomatoes**
- **1 yellow squash**
- **2 celery stalks**
- **10 fresh green beans**

- **5 fresh sage leaves**
- **3 cups water**
- **1 6-ounce can Hunt's tomato paste**
- **1 tablespoon thyme or Italian herb mix**
- **Sea salt and pepper to taste**
- **1 15-ounce can cannellini beans**
- **1 cup uncooked elbow macaroni**
- **1 loaf rustic bread**

THE MOVES

1. Chop garlic, onion, carrots, zucchini, tomatoes (reserve juice), squash, and celery.

2. Snap the ends off of the green beans and cut into thirds.

3. In a large pot over medium heat, heat olive oil.

4. Add garlic, onion, and sage and sauté for 3-5 minutes or until onions start to sweat.

5. Add carrots, zucchini, tomatoes, squash, celery, and green beans. Stir well.

6. Add water, tomato paste, thyme or Italian herbs, salt, and pepper. Stir together mixing well.

7. Bring to a boil then turn down to medium low.

8. Add the can of beans and the liquid, cover and let simmer for at least 30 minutes.

9. Ten minutes before serving, add macaroni and stir well.

10. Slice and toast rustic bread. Serve warm alongside soup.

Serves 2

Cream of Wild Mushroom Soup

If you love mushrooms, then you'll love this soup. The girls I date have to like mushrooms. There's a big difference between a person who would choose a pepperoni pizza over a mushroom pizza.

> 1 pound assorted wild mushrooms
>
> 1 small onion
>
> 1/2 stick butter (4 tablespoons)
>
> 1 teaspoon rosemary, thyme, or any herb mix
>
> 1 tablespoon flour
>
> 2 15-ounce cans chicken broth
>
> 1 cup cream
>
> Salt and pepper to taste

THE MOVES

1. Clean the mushrooms with a paper towel, cut off stems, and chop.

2. Chop the onion.

3. In a soup pot melt the butter over medium heat.

4. Add the mushrooms, onion, and herbs. Cook over low heat for 10 minutes, stirring frequently.

5. Add the flour into the pot, stirring to combine well.

6. Add the broth and bring to a boil. Reduce heat to low and simmer for 15-20 minutes.

7. Add the cream and salt and pepper to taste. Simmer for another 10 minutes before serving.

Serves 2

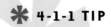 **4-1-1 TIP**
Save 1 fresh mushroom, cut lengthwise, and use as a garnish for the soup.

Potato Soup

Here's the basic version. I'll let you use your creativity regarding what else you want to throw into it. Always look at all your options because as long as you have options, you have choices.

{
- **1 small onion**
- **4 medium potatoes**
- **2 tablespoons butter**
- **1 cup chicken broth**
- **2 tablespoons dried parsley**
- **Pinch of dried thyme**
- **Salt and pepper to taste**
- **1 1/2 cups milk**
- **2 tablespoons flour**

THE MOVES

1. Chop the onion. Peel and dice the potatoes.

2. Heat a large soup pot over medium heat. Add butter and onions and sauté until soft.

3. Add potatoes, broth, parsley, thyme, salt, and pepper to the pot. Simmer for 15 minutes over medium heat, stirring occasionally.

4. In a separate bowl, combine milk and flour and stir until well mixed. Pour the milk mixture into the soup. Stir until thickened.

5. Simmer for another 10 minutes before serving.

Serves 2

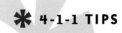

✳ 4-1-1 TIPS

* You can throw in some ham, leeks, or bacon pieces, too.
* You can also puree half of the soup in a blender and then add it back to the main soup.

Birds *of* a Feather

YOU HAVE SO MUCH IN COMMON, you're birds of a feather. How cute! You wear the same brand of clothes, drink the same drinks, and love the dark meat.

Chicken and turkey are great sources of protein and are really easy to work with. The two most important things you have to remember about poultry are: always wash your bird, and make sure it's cooked through until the meat on the inside has no pink. Otherwise, you'll be committing a serious "party fowl" and probably will be single again.

WHAT'S HOT? • *Ostrich Meat* • *Spices* • *Ground Turkey*

Tandoori Chicken

The flavors in Indian food are intense. You won't need an earthen tandoor oven for this recipe; your regular oven or grill will do the trick. You can buy pre-made Tandoori spice mix in most stores now or make your own. I've included the recipe.

1 cup plain yogurt

1/2 cup honey

Tandoori spice

Juice of 1/2 lemon

4-6 pieces boneless, skinless chicken breasts

Tandoori Spice:

1 teaspoon black pepper

2 teaspoons ground cumin

1 teaspoon coriander seeds

1 teaspoon ground or crushed cloves

1 teaspoon turmeric

2 teaspoons paprika

1 teaspoon cayenne pepper or red chili powder

1 teaspoon cinnamon

1 teaspoon nutmeg

1 teaspoon salt

THE MOVES

1. In a mixing bowl combine all of the ingredients for the tandoori spice. Mix well.

2. In a large bowl combine the yogurt, honey, tandoori spice, and lemon juice together to make the marinade.

3. Add the chicken pieces and coat well. Cover and marinate in the refrigerator for at least an hour. Two hours is better, and overnight is best.

4. Grill over high heat for 10 minutes per side or until cooked through. (The chicken can also be baked in an ovenproof pan. First sear the chicken pieces for about 2-3 minutes over high heat, and then transfer the pan to a 350 degree F oven and bake for 20 minutes or until cooked through.)

Serves 2-4

 4-1-1 TIP

You can use any part of the chicken for this dish. This is a perfect time to ask what your date's favorite piece of the chicken is— and use that. What if it's not your favorite piece? That's called adaptation, my friend.

Pan Roasted Almond Crusted Chicken

Almonds are really high in fiber and good for your skin and nails. (Guys, don't tell your boys this because they might think you're metro.) Almonds give chicken a nice crunchy bite. Try flavored almonds, like Blue Diamond Almonds, to give the chicken a tangy or spicy bite.

{
1 cup almonds, shelled

2 teaspoons paprika

Sea salt and pepper to taste

2 large egg whites

4 boneless, skinless chicken breasts

1 tablespoon extra virgin olive oil

1 tablespoon butter melted

THE MOVES

1. Preheat the oven to 350 degrees F.

2. Finely chop the almonds in a food processor or blender. Transfer to a shallow dish and stir in the paprika, salt, and pepper.

3. Whisk the egg whites in another shallow bowl.

4. Dip each piece of chicken into the egg, letting the excess drip back into the dish. Then press both sides of the chicken into the nut mixture and coat thoroughly.

5. In a medium-size ovenproof skillet over medium heat warm the oil and the butter. Cook the chicken until the nuts set and turn golden brown, about 3 to 4 minutes per side.

6. Transfer the pan into the oven and bake until cooked through, about 20 minutes.

Serves 2

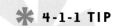 **4-1-1 TIP**

To set the almond crust, chill it in the fridge for at least 20 minutes.

Holiday Turkey

It's important to brine your turkey for at least 2 hours, preferably over night, which makes it juicer and more flavorful. You need a container large enough to hold your turkey during the brining process and enough brine to cover it. You'll also need enough room to refrigerate it. A lady told me she brined her turkey in the bathtub. I don't recommend that. That's a bad visual.

> **1 cup sea salt, per gallon**
>
> **1/2 cup juice, per gallon (apple, orange, or pineapple)**
>
> **6 cloves garlic, peeled and minced, per gallon**
>
> **1 cup dried herb mix, per gallon**

COOKING A TURKEY: FRESH VS. FROZEN

I prefer fresh turkeys versus frozen. Buy a fresh turkey 1–2 days before the holiday. Keep it in the refrigerator in a high-sided pan to catch juices that may leak from it.

If you buy a frozen turkey, thaw it in the refrigerator. One day of thawing is required per 5 pounds, so plan ahead. A 20-pound turkey will take 4 days to completely thaw out.

To ensure proper cooking, have a meat thermometer on hand to check for doneness.

THE MOVES

1. Preheat oven to 325 degrees F.

2. Remove the turkey from the brine and place it breast up on a flat wire rack in a shallow baking pan (2-3 inches deep).

3. Tuck the wings back under the shoulders and add 1/2 cup of the brine to the bottom of the pan. Place a foil tent loosely over the turkey.

4. Bake the turkey for 1 hour and then remove the foil tent so that the turkey can brown. Baste the turkey every 45 minutes to keep it moist.

5. When the turkey is fully cooked (see approximate cooking times below), remove it from the oven, place it on a cutting board, and let it sit for 10 minutes before carving. A turkey is fully cooked when it reaches an internal temperature of 165 degrees F. Insert the meat thermometer into the thickest part of the thigh to check the internal temperature.

Approximate cooking times:

Weight	Un-stuffed
14–18 pounds	3 1/2 –4 1/2 hours
18–20	4–4 1/2 hours
20–24	4 1/2–5 hours

Cordon Bleu Chicken Breasts

This is a traditional, old-school way of making chicken. You can never go wrong with this dish. Oh yeah—get out your big wood pounder because it's time to pummel your chicken.

{
4 boneless, skinless chicken breasts

Salt and pepper to taste

4 slices ham

4 slices Swiss or provolone cheese

1/4 cup flour

1 egg

1 cup Italian breadcrumbs

1/2 stick butter

1/2 cup chicken broth

1/2 cup tomato sauce

THE MOVES

1. Preheat oven to 350 degrees F.

2. Pound the hell out of the chicken and get rid of all those nervous feelings about actually making this dish for your date. Pound to about 1/4-inch thickness.

3. Sprinkle with salt and pepper.

4. Put 1 slice of ham and 1 slice of cheese on each chicken breast.

5. Roll up each breast with the cheese and ham in the center. If needed, secure with a toothpick.

6. Whisk the egg. Arrange three shallow bowls, one with the whisked egg, one with the flour, and one with the breadcrumbs.

7. Dredge the chicken pieces in the flour, then dunk them in the egg, and then in the breadcrumbs.

8. Place the chicken seam side down in a shallow baking dish. Pour tomato sauce over the chicken and bake 30 minutes or until cooked through.

Serves 2-4

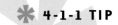 **4-1-1 TIP**

To add a deeper, more robust flavor, use Serrano ham or prosciutto ham.

Mushroom and White Wine Chicken

This recipe really brings out the natural flavor of the chicken. I like the taste of chicken, so I don't like drowning it with big heavy sauces. This recipe is nice and light, and you can use the wine that you're already drinking.

{

1 tablespoon vegetable oil

2-5 cloves garlic, peeled and chopped

1 large shallot, finely chopped

4 boneless, skinless chicken breasts

4 cups mushrooms, sliced

1 cup white wine (use whatever you are drinking)

1 teaspoon Dijon mustard

2 tablespoons dried thyme

Salt and pepper to taste

THE MOVES

1. In a large skillet over medium heat add vegetable oil, garlic, and shallot.

2. Add chicken to the skillet and brown on each side.

3. Add mushrooms, white wine, mustard, thyme, salt, and pepper.

4. Cook for 3-5 minutes or until mushrooms are soft.

5. Bring to a boil, stirring frequently, then set to simmer, cover, and cook for 20-25 minutes.

Serves 2-4

 4-1-1 TIPS

* For the mushrooms you can use cremini, baby Portobello, or white. Or mix it up, and use a combo of shroomies.

* Some good white wines to use for this dish are Pinot Grigio and Chablis, which are white wines aged in a steel barrel. A Chardonnay is also good because of the oak flavor from aging in oak barrels.

* This dish is also good served over rice or pasta.

Spicy Baked Chicken in Chipotle Sauce

This is a nice way to get a little spice in your life. Chipotles are smoked jalapeños, and they can be found everywhere now. They are canned with adobo sauce, and I recommend using the whole can, sauce and all.

1/2 stick butter

1/4 cup red wine

1 tablespoon Worcestershire sauce

1 4-ounce can chipotle chiles in adobo sauce, chopped

1 clove garlic, minced

Salt and pepper to taste

4 boneless, skinless chicken breasts, cut into cubes

THE MOVES

1. Preheat oven to 400 degrees F.

2. Over medium heat melt butter in large ovenproof skillet.

3. Add wine, Worcestershire sauce, chipotles, garlic, salt, and pepper, stirring for about 1 minute.

4. Add chicken to the skillet and toss until well coated. Cook for 2 minutes.

5. Transfer the skillet to the oven and bake 15-20 minutes or until chicken is cooked through.

Serves 2-4

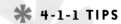
4-1-1 TIPS

* Serve with a sliced baguette.
* This dish is good served over white or brown rice.

Honey and Horseradish Chicken Thighs

The honey gives the chicken a sweet bite, while the horsey-sauce gives it a tangy bite.
This crazy blend goes great with dark meat.

{
1/4 cup water

1/2 cup honey

1/2 cup horseradish mustard

1-2 pounds chicken thighs

THE MOVES

1. Preheat oven to 350 degrees F or fire up the 'cue.

2. In a large saucepan combine the water, honey, and mustard. Simmer over medium low heat for about 5 minutes, stirring frequently.

3. Add the chicken to the saucepan and coat well to get all those flavors fused together.

4. Transfer chicken to a shallow baking dish and place in the oven. Bake for 30 minutes or until cooked through.

5. Pour the extra sauce over the chicken while it is cooking for added flavor.

Serves 2-4

Rosemary's Chicken

This isn't like Rosemary's baby, so don't worry about the devil coming out of the chicken. This chicken is pure herb heaven.

4 large boneless, skinless chicken breast halves

1/4 cup French's classic yellow mustard

1/4 cup orange juice

2 tablespoons cider vinegar

2 teaspoons rosemary leaves, minced

4 strips bacon

Toothpicks

THE MOVES

1. Place chicken in a large, sealable plastic bag.

2. Add the mustard, orange juice, vinegar, and rosemary into the plastic bag, seal and mix well. Marinate in the fridge for at least 30 minutes.

3. Preheat grill.

4. Wrap 1 strip of bacon around each piece of chicken and secure with a toothpick.

5. Grill chicken over medium heat for 25 minutes or until cooked through. Baste the chicken repeatedly while cooking with the leftover marinade, making sure the chicken is cooked well after the final application of marinade.

Serves 2-4

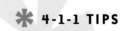

✳ 4-1-1 TIPS

* The longer you can marinate the better.
* Don't forget to remove the toothpicks before serving— or I hope you know the Heimlich.

Baked Lemon-Mustard Chicken Breasts

This is a healthy way to eat chicken when you want to relax at home and eat a satisfying meal.

{
- **1/4 cup Grey Poupon Dijon mustard**
- **Juice of 1 lemon**
- **2-4 skinless, boneless chicken breasts**
- **1 teaspoon olive oil**
- **Salt and pepper to taste**

THE MOVES

1. Preheat oven to 450 degrees F.

2. In a medium bowl mix the mustard and lemon juice.

3. Pierce the chicken with a fork or knife and add to the bowl.

4. Place foil in a shallow baking dish. Evenly spread the olive oil on the foil.

5. Place the chicken breasts in the baking dish and pour the rest of the marinade over them.

6. Bake for 30-45 minutes or until cooked through.

Serves 2-4

Hog Heaven

I KNOW YOU LIKE MUD MASKS and getting pampered. So when a pig does it, don't consider it dirty. It's like getting a full-body mud mask.

It's said that pork is the other white meat, and it's becoming so popular with Americans that there might soon be a tie between pork and chicken in terms of how much we eat every year. Most popular is the pork chop, and the most tender is the tenderloin.

WHAT'S HOT? • *Cooking pork slow-n-low* • *Memphis, Tennessee*
• *Eating with your fingers without using wet naps—South Carolina-style*

Pork and Pineapple Skewers

Any sweet fruit works well with pork, not just pineapple. Get creative and try these skewers using orange slices or mango slices.

{
- **4 boneless, skinless chicken breasts**
- **2 tablespoons brown sugar**
- **2 teaspoons vegetable oil**
- **1 teaspoon mustard**
- **1/2 pound cooked ham, cut into 1-inch cubes**
- **1 15-ounce can pineapple chunks, drained**
- **4 skewers, bamboo or steel**

THE MOVES

1. Preheat grill on high.

2. In a medium bowl mix together brown sugar, vegetable oil, and mustard.

3. Spear ham and pineapple chunks alternately onto skewers (if using wooden skewers, soak them in water for a few minutes first).

4. Place skewers on the grill, and brush liberally with the brown sugar sauce. Cook for 5-10 minutes, turning frequently and basting often.

Serves 2

Far East Spareribs

I cook these every year for my Aunt Janice for her birthday. The trick is to marinate them overnight in the Far East sauce. This will make them sweet, tender, and juicy.

> **1/2 cup honey**
>
> **Juice of 1 lemon**
>
> **1/2 cup soy sauce**
>
> **Pepper to taste**
>
> **1-3 pounds spareribs, individually cut**

THE MOVES

1. In a large, sealable plastic bag, add honey, lemon, soy sauce, and pepper. Mix well.

2. Add ribs to the bag and seal. Mix together until ribs are well coated. Put the bag in the refrigerator and marinate overnight.

3. Grill the spareribs over medium high heat for 10 minutes or until cooked through and nice and crispy.

Serves 2-4

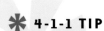 **✳ 4-1-1 TIP**

If you don't have a grill, you can bake the ribs in the oven at 350 degrees F for 20 minutes or until cooked through. For crispy ribs, put them under the broiler for 2 minutes more.

Champagne Ham

This is a big piece of ham to cook up. But it's worth it because of how tasty those sandwiches made with the leftovers are going to taste all week.

{
1 5-pound boneless ham

1 bottle champagne

1/2 cup honey

1 cup brown sugar

THE MOVES

1. Preheat oven to 300 degrees F.

2. Score ham and place in baking pan.

3. Pour half of the champagne over ham.

4. Rub the honey all over the ham to coat, then sprinkle with the brown sugar.

5. Bake for 2 hours then pour the remaining champagne over the ham and cook for another 30 minutes, basting the ham every 10 minutes during the final 30 minutes.

Serves 4

Pan Roasted Pork Chops *with* White Wine & Garlic Cheese Sauce

This dish is good with rice because it absorbs all the extra sauce.

{
- 1/2 tablespoon butter
- 3-5 cloves garlic, minced
- 2-4 pork chops
- Salt and pepper to taste
- 1/2 cup white wine (use whatever you're drinking)
- 2 cups cooked brown or white rice
- 1/2 cup Parmesan cheese

THE MOVES

1. Preheat oven to 350 degrees F.

2. Heat an ovenproof pan on the stove over high heat.

3. Add butter and garlic to the pan and sauté until butter is melted.

4. Season pork chops with salt and pepper and add to the pan. Cook on one side for about 1 minute and then flip. Cook for another minute.

5. Add wine and bring to a boil. Transfer the pan to the oven and cook for 10 minutes or until pork is cooked through.

6. Serve the pork chops over the rice and then pour the remaining juice on top. Sprinkle the Parmesan cheese on the pork chops and around the plate.

Serves 2-4

APHRODISIAC #8: Almonds

A symbol of fertility throughout the ages, the aroma is thought to induce passion in a female. Try serving marzipan (almond paste) in the shapes of fruits for a special after-dinner treat.

APHRODISIAC #9: Mustard

It is believed that mustard stimulates the sex glands and increases desire.

APHRODISIAC #10: Wine and Champagne

A glass (or four) of wine or champagne can greatly enhance a romantic interlude. They help stimulate our senses, and drinking them can be an erotic experience. Caress the glass and savor the taste on your lips. But remember that excessive alcohol will make you too drowsy for that after-dinner romance, so don't get too tipsy and make a fool of yourself.

APHRODISIAC #11: Honey

Egyptians used honey as a cure for sterility and impotence. Lovers on their "honeymoon" drank honey-based teas because it was thought to sweeten the marriage.

Baked Ham *with* Honey, Brown Sugar, and Mustard Glaze

If you take this to a holiday party, you will make some new cousins for life. What's the other great thing about this dish? Leftovers!

{
- **1/2 cup honey**
- **1/2 cup brown sugar**
- **1/2 cup brown mustard**
- **Juice of 1 orange**
- **1 5-10 pound ham shank, bone in and skin on**

THE MOVES

1. Preheat oven to 350 degrees F.

2. In a large bowl combine honey, brown sugar, mustard, and orange juice.

3. Score the ham in a diamond pattern, but don't pierce the meat. Put the ham into a medium to large baking pan.

4. Bake the ham on the middle rack for 2 hours, then pull it out and rub the glaze all over it. Cover with foil so the bone won't burn, and cook another 2 hours.

Serves 5-10

 4-1-1 TIPS

* If you want to use a meat thermometer to check if the ham is cooked, place it in the thickest part of the ham. The ham is cooked when the thermometer reaches 165 degrees.

* Ginger and orange peel can be added to the rub for an extra bite.

* Always let meat rest after it is done cooking for about 5 minutes to keep it juicy.

Parmesan Pork Chops Dijon

If pork is the other white meat, then I guess Dijon is the other French mustard. The two together…hmmm, can you say pork heaven? The mustard gives this dish a nice tangy kick that goes great with the tenderness of the pork.

{
1/2 cup Dijon mustard

4 tablespoons Italian dressing

2 tablespoons Parmesan cheese

1/4 teaspoon pepper

2 pork chops, approximately 1/2-inch-thick

1 tablespoon olive oil

THE MOVES

1. Preheat oven to 350 degrees F.

2. In a medium bowl combine the mustard, dressing, cheese, and pepper.

3. Add the pork chops and coat well.

4. Grease a baking dish with the olive oil.

5. Place pork chops in the baking dish and bake for 12-15 minutes or until cooked through.

Serves 2-4

Meathead

DID YOU KNOW THAT DATING A MEATHEAD is always better than dating no one? Don't fret; you can always make your date eat a veggie once in a while. This section is for all the meat lovers out there. I know your philosophy is the bigger the piece of meat, the better. But small and savory works, too.

When you haven't had meat in awhile and you want to splurge, or you're a meat enthusiast, try some of these recipes to get a new and refreshing meat fix.

WHAT'S HOT? • *Flat-iron steaks* • *Buffalo burgers*
• *Rival Crock-pots and Dutch ovens*

Deviled Top Sirloin Steak

This dish will bring out the devil in your date for sure. It's good to be bad once in a while. Just make sure you have a cold drink handy for when your date gets all fired up.

- 2 tablespoons catsup
- 1/2 cup red wine
- 2 tablespoons Sriracha chili sauce, or your favorite hot chili sauce
- 1 tablespoon Worcestershire sauce
- Garlic salt and pepper to taste
- 2 top sirloin steaks

THE MOVES

1. In a large bowl combine the catsup, red wine, chili sauce, woosy sauce, salt, and pepper.

2. Add the steaks, cover, and marinate in the refrigerator for 30 minutes.

3. Grill the steaks over a high flame, basting with the excess marinade until desired doneness, making sure the steak is well cooked after the last application of marinade.

Serves 2

Steak Topper

Try this quick little combo-of-love as a topper for most any steak.

- 2 tablespoons oil
- 2 cloves garlic, peeled and chopped
- 5 mushrooms, chopped
- 1/2 small onion, chopped
- 1/4 cup A-1 sauce

THE MOVES

1. Heat the oil in a small saucepan over medium heat.

2. Combine all the ingredients in the saucepan and sauté for 10 minutes or until desired thickness is achieved.

3. Pour over cooked steak.

Serves 2

Beef and Broccoli

Here's a nice Asian twist for you Meatheads. Use whatever cut of meat you like. I try to find good cuts that are on sale. Shop smart! Grocery stores sometimes have pre-cut cubes of meat.

1 tablespoon olive oil

1 pound steak, cut into thin, 1-inch slices

1 head broccoli

1/2 cup soy sauce

1 tablespoon rice vinegar

1 teaspoon sesame oil

Pepper to taste

THE MOVES

1. In a large pan heat olive oil over medium high heat.

2. Rinse the broccoli. Cut the florets from the head of broccoli and set aside.

3. To the pan add steak, broccoli, soy sauce, rice vinegar, sesame oil, and pepper. Mix all ingredients coating the steak and broccoli well.

4. Cook until broccoli is tender and meat is cooked until desired doneness.

Serves 2

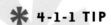

✳ 4-1-1 TIP

Add a chopped chile pepper for a tongue-blazing experience.

Hook-Up Hamburger

*This is a protein-style burger with no carbs because there is no bun.
You can also use ground turkey, ground ostrich, or ground buffalo.
Buffalo and ostrich are high in protein and have no saturated fat.*

{

1 pound ground beef, shaped into two flat patties (not golf balls)

2 Portobello mushrooms

2 cups mixed field greens, washed and dried

1/2 cup salad dressing of your choice

1/2 cup Parmesan cheese

2 tomato slices from a large tomato

1 bulb roasted garlic, optional

THE MOVES

1. Grill the burgers to your liking. I recommend medium-well.

2. When the burgers are almost done, grill the Portobello mushrooms until they are soft.

3. In a medium bowl combine the field greens, dressing, and Parmesan cheese. Toss well.

4. Now build your protein burger: On a plate, add 1 cup of the salad, then the burger, tomato, and mushroom. Sprinkle with more Parmesan cheese and roasted garlic, if using.

Serves 2

 4-1-1 TIPS

* Balsamic vinaigrette, Russian dressing, and Italian dressing work best.

* You can also add your favorite cheese to the burgers. Brie, pepper Jack, and blue cheese work nicely.

Porterhouse and Blue Cheese Rafts

The trick with grilling or broiling steaks with cheese is to put each steak in a foil wrap like a shiny raft that can't leak around the edges. If you are one of those balloon animal makers, you can create a goose out of the foil.

- **2 (6-10 ounce) steaks**
- **Garlic salt and pepper to taste**
- **1 cup crumbled blue cheese**
- **2 teaspoons Worcestershire sauce**
- **2 teaspoons A-1 steak sauce**

THE MOVES

1. Preheat grill to 400 degrees F.
2. Place each steak on a sheet of foil.
3. Season the steaks with the garlic salt and pepper.
4. Spread 1/2 cup of cheese on each steak.
5. Pour Worcestershire sauce and A-1 sauce over steaks.
6. Wrap foil securing around each steak, sealing all the corners so they don't leak and sink your steak.
7. Grill the steaks for 10 minutes, flipping once at the halfway point.
8. Let the steaks rest for a few minutes before serving.

Serves 2

Classy Pot Roast

With this recipe it's all about slow-n-low, like all day slow. What's great is that the prep can be done the night before, and then in the morning you just have to put the roast in the Crock-pot.

{
1 tablespoon olive oil

1 tablespoon salt

1 tablespoon pepper

1 1-2 pound boneless chuck roast

1 large onion, chopped

1 cup red wine

2 tablespoons dried thyme

5 cloves garlic, chopped

1 15-ounce can beef broth

1 bay leaf

3 carrots, cut into 1-inch pieces

3 Yukon gold potatoes, cubed

THE MOVES

Crock-pot:

1. Plug in Crock-pot and set to low.
2. Add oil to Crock-pot.
3. Rinse pot roast, pat dry, and season with salt and pepper.
4. Add roast, onions, red wine, thyme, and garlic to Crock-pot.
5. Add beef broth, carrots, and potatoes.
6. Put on the lid and cook all day (8-9 hours).

Dutch Oven:

1. Preheat oven to 350 degrees F.
2. Heat olive oil in the Dutch oven over medium high heat.
3. Rinse pot roast, pat dry, and season with salt and pepper. In the Dutch oven, brown the roast on all sides.
4. Add onions, red wine, thyme, garlic, beef broth, bay leaf, carrots, and potatoes. Bring to a boil and then take off stove.
5. Put the lid on and transfer to the oven.
6. Cook for 2-3 hours or until tender.

Serves 2-4

✳ 4-1-1 TIPS

* A Dutch oven is a large, deep pan with thick walls and a tight-fitting lid. It is designed to be transferred from the stovetop to the oven, and it is usually made of cast iron. It locks in the heat and moisture for a very tender cooking experience.

* Don't cut the meat when done; instead, shred it using 2 forks.

Pepper Crusted Steaks
with Garlic Chive Butter

Holy hot date, Batman! This is a serious steak with a lots of flavors and layers going on. Oh, I'll say it: flavor layers. It's a great, cheesy "buzz word." Some of this steak can be saved for breakfast to make steak and eggs.

{
2 6-10 ounce steaks

1 tablespoon pepper

1/2 stick butter (4 tablespoons)

1 shallot, finely chopped

2-4 garlic cloves, finely chopped

1 tablespoon chives

THE MOVES

1. Preheat grill to 400 degrees F.

2. Season the steaks by rubbing the pepper evenly over both sides.

3. In a medium saucepan over medium heat, sauté butter, shallots, garlic, and chives.

4. Place the steaks on the grill and pour half of the butter sauce over them. Grill until desired doneness.

5. Serve the steaks with the remaining butter sauce on top.

Serves 2

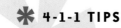

✳ 4-1-1 TIPS

* T-bone steaks and New York strip steaks work really well.

* If you had this steak at a restaurant it would cost $35.00!

* For a creative twist, use white pepper instead of black pepper.

Mindless Meatloaf

Why does meatloaf always sound so complicated? You blend ground meat together with veggies and herbs, mold it, and cook. It couldn't be simpler. If you can't make this meatloaf, I suggest you move back in with your parents and start collecting government checks.

{
2 tablespoons olive oil

1 medium onion, diced

5 cloves garlic, minced

1 tablespoon herb mix

1 pound lean ground beef

1/2 cup breadcrumbs

1 large egg

1/2 cup Parmesan cheese

1 teaspoon Worcestershire sauce

Salt and pepper to taste

1 cup tomato sauce

THE MOVES

1. Preheat oven to 350 degrees F.

2. In a medium pan over medium heat add olive oil, onion, garlic, and herbs. Sauté for 3-4 minutes.

3. In a large bowl combine ground beef, breadcrumbs, egg, Parmesan cheese, Worcestershire sauce, salt, pepper and 1/2 of the tomato sauce. Mix well.

4. Add sautéed onion mixture to the meat mixture and mix all ingredients well. Using your hands works really well.

5. Transfer to a loaf dish. Pour the remaining tomato sauce on top of the loaf.

6. Bake for 45 minutes or until center is brown or has reached a temp of 160 degrees F.

Serves 2-4

WHAT'S HOT? • *Wild salmon* • *Cedar planks for cooking fish on the barbecue* • *Asian flavors*

Something's Fishy

WHEN YOU COOK AND EAT FISH, your date will automatically think you're in shape and healthy. Do you know why the Japanese and people that live in the Mediterranean region live the longest? They eat a lot of fish. The oils in fish, Omega 3 oils, are great for your heart. Add wine with that and you'll live and love forever.

A tip on buying fish: When you buy fish at the market, it's not supposed to smell like fish. Fresh fish smells like the ocean or has no smell at all. *So smell your fish before you buy it.*

Bacon Wrapped Tropical Scallops

Here's my crunchy twist to scallops. What's great about scallops is they are like sponges—they suck up everything. So the trick is to not let them marinate too long; just about five minutes is best. If you leave them soaking too long they get soggy.

The flavors of the fruit along with the crunchiness of the bacon and warm honey glaze makes this scallop recipe burst with flavor.

1/2 cup pineapple juice	**Toothpicks or wooden skewers**
1/2 cup orange juice	**2 tablespoons honey**
1 pound scallops, rinsed and dried	**2 tablespoons olive oil**
1/4 pound bacon	**Salt and pepper to taste**

THE MOVES

1. Combine the pineapple and orange juice and stir well.

2. Marinate scallops in a shallow dish with tropical juice blend for about 5 minutes.

3. Remove scallops from the juice and wrap a slice of bacon around each one, piercing with a toothpick where the two ends of bacon overlap.

4. Set the oven to broil.

5. In a small bowl combine honey, olive oil, salt, and pepper. Whisk well. Brush the honey/oil mixture onto the bacon and scallops.

6. Place scallops on a baking sheet and broil for 4-5 minutes per side or until crispy. You can also pan fry them for about the same amount of time.

Serves 2-4

✳ 4-1-1 TIPS

* Either the pineapple juice or orange juice can be substituted with mango juice for a slightly different flavor.

* Wooden skewers should always be soaked in water for a few minutes before using.

* Scallops are usually soaked in a water solution so they will keep longer. This makes them very wet and hard to sauté. If you get wet scallops, it is best to grill them. Ask for dry scallops, which will be easier to sauté, and they taste better.

Salmon Pita *with* Olive Tapenade and Wild Field Greens

This is one of my favorite recipes because it's really delicious yet simple. All the simple flavors in this recipe add up to a big flavor blast. The olives, avocado, and salmon work together in perfect flavor harmony while the field greens give it a nice crunch.

{
2 6-ounce salmon fillets, de-fleshed and grilled.

2 whole pitas

4 tablespoons olive tapenade spread

1 bag wild field greens, rinsed and dried

1 avocado, skin removed and diced

1/2 cup balsamic vinaigrette

Salt and pepper to taste

THE MOVES

1. Cut each cooked salmon fillet in half lengthwise.

2. Warm the pitas over the grill or on the stove.

3. Once the pitas are warm, cut them in half. Spread the olive tapenade inside each pita half on each side.

4. Combine the field greens, avocado, and balsamic vinaigrette.

5. Stuff each pita half with 1 piece of salmon and an equal portion of the field greens mixture.

Serves 2

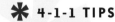

✻ 4-1-1 TIPS

* You can buy olive tapenade at specialty grocery stores such as Trader Joe's and Whole Foods. Tapenade is pulsed olives with olive oil.

* This sandwich is also good eaten cold.

* If you're making this sandwich to take on a picnic or other outing, make sure to wait and mix the greens and the vinaigrette until the last moment because otherwise the greens will get soggy.

Firecracker Shrimp *with* Cajun Salmon Butter

This dish has some heat to it, but it's a full-flavor heat, not the, "Oh my God, I've burned my date's lips off!" The heat comes from a cayenne pepper sauce I use to help bring out the essence of the shrimp. Make sure to have a lot of paper towels handy because eating this dish can get messy.

{
- **1 pound uncooked shrimp, shelled and de-veined**
- **1/2 cup Frank's RedHot Sauce**
- **Salt and pepper to taste**
- **4 tablespoons butter**
- **7 ounces Salads of the Sea Cajun Smoked Salmon**

THE MOVES

1. In a strainer, rinse the shrimp well under cold water.

2. In a large bowl combine the shrimp, Frank's RedHot Sauce, salt, and pepper. Cover and marinate for 30 minutes in the refrigerator.

3. In a large pan over medium heat melt the butter. Add the Cajun smoked salmon and stir together.

4. Add shrimp to the pan and sauté for about 7-10 minutes or until shrimp turns pink and is cooked through.

5. Dig in and eat this as a finger food, or put it over rice.

Serves 2

Real Maryland Lump Crab Cakes

An ex-girlfriend made these for me, and she's from Maryland. Of course, when we broke up, she wouldn't give me the recipe, so I had to figure it out on my own. They are the tastiest crab cakes I've ever made. The trick is to not use a lot of filler. It's all about the lump crab meat.

2 slices of bread, crusts removed and torn into small pieces

1 large egg, beaten

2 tablespoons mayonnaise

1 teaspoon Worcestershire sauce

1 teaspoon French's yellow mustard

2 teaspoons fresh parsley, chopped

2 teaspoons Old Bay seasoning

1 pound Phillips lump crab meat

THE MOVES

1. Set the oven to broil.
2. In a large mixing bowl combine bread, egg, mayonnaise, Worcestershire sauce, mustard, parsley, and Old Bay seasoning. Blend well.
3. Stir in the crab meat, folding gently but still mix thoroughly.
4. Shape into nice, thick crab cakes (about 4 inches in diameter).
5. Broil for about 10 minutes until the top is nice and crispy.

Serves 2-4

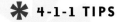

✳ 4-1-1 TIPS

* Broiling is the best way to get the perfect crab cake, but you can also pan fry them in a 1 tablespoon of butter.
* You can also make these ahead and freeze them for use later.
* 1 cup of breadcrumbs can be substituted for the fresh bread pieces.

Fish Tacos

I eat fish tacos for breakfast, lunch, and dinner everytime I go to Mexico. My only concern about the ones I ate there was that the fish was always deep fried. I like the taste of fish, so I thought it altered the true flavor of a Baja-style fish taco. Being the independent guy I am, I created my own fish taco. This is my healthier version of the traditional.

{
1 pound white fish fillets

2 tablespoons olive oil

Salt and pepper to taste

1 lemon, cut in half

1 head of cabbage, finely chopped

1/2 cup mayonnaise

4 tablespoons Sriracha chili sauce

1 12-ounce can of refried beans

4 corn tortillas

THE MOVES

1. Rinse the fish fillets in cold water and pat dry. Rub the oil on both sides.

2. Season the fillets with salt and pepper on both sides.

3. Grill the fillets for about 5 minutes on each side or until crispy and flaky.

4. Squeeze the juice from the lemon on the fillets while they are grilling.

5. In the meantime, heat the refried beans on the stove or in the microwave.

6. Remove the cooked fillets from the grill and cut them into 1/2-inch strips.

7. Chop the cabbage and put in a mixing bowl. Add the mayonnaise and chili sauce to the cabbage. Mix together.

8. Warm the tortillas on the grill.

9. On each tortilla, spread a spoonful of beans, then add several strips of fish, and top with the cabbage blend.

Serves 2-4

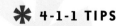

✳ 4-1-1 TIPS

* Halibut works best for fish tacos, but you can really use any white fish.

* Guacamole is also a great fish taco topping.

Far East Shrimp over Rice

Shrimp has such a nice, delicate flavor. The goal is to enhance that flavor, not disguise or drown it with a big heavy sauce. Always remember, less is more with fish. (Just like telling your date your life story: less is more.)

> 2 tablespoons soy sauce
>
> 2 bags instant brown rice, cooked
>
> 2 tablespoons rice wine vinegar
>
> Juice of 1 lemon
>
> 2 tablespoons honey
>
> 1 pound uncooked shrimp, peeled and de-veined

THE MOVES

1. Heat a large saucepan over medium heat. Add the soy sauce, rice wine vinegar, lemon juice, and honey. Stir until blended well.

2. In a strainer rinse the shrimp well under cold water then add them to the saucepan.

3. Sauté the shrimp for 8-10 minutes or until they are pink and cooked through.

4. Arrange the rice on a plate or in a bowl and pour the shrimp and sauce over it.

Serves 2-4

Pan Fried Tangerine Sole

This recipe gives this versatile fish a clean and tangy flavor. You can use any white fish. But if you can get your hands on petrale sole, hold on tight, cause that is the best.

> 1/2 cup tangerine juice
>
> 1 cup panko breadcrumbs
>
> 2 eggs, beaten
>
> 1 tablespoon olive oil
>
> 1 pound sole fillets
>
> Sea salt and pepper to taste

THE MOVES

1. Put the juice, the breadcrumbs, and the egg in 3 separate, shallow bowls.

2. Heat the oil in a large skillet over medium heat.

3. Take the fillets and dip in the juice, then the egg, then the breadcrumbs.

4. Add fish to the hot skillet and cook for about 3 minutes on each side or until crispy on the outside and flaky on the inside.

5. Season with salt and pepper to taste.

Serves 2-4

Blackened Tuna *with* Mustard, Soy Sauce, and Sesame Seeds

The trick when cooking the tuna is to sear it on the outside while leaving the center pink and raw. With tuna, you just want the edges cooked and blackened.

1 teaspoon olive oil

1 pound fresh tuna, about 2 inches thick

1 cup black pepper

1/4 cup Colman's mustard powder or Dijon Mustard

1/4 cup soy sauce

2 tablespoons sesame seeds

THE MOVES

1. Heat a large skillet over medium high heat.

2. Rinse the fish and pat dry. Rub the fish with the oil.

3. Sprinkle the black pepper evenly over both sides of the fish.

4. In a medium bowl combine the mustard, soy sauce, and sesame seeds.

5. Put fish in the skillet and sear for about 1 minute. Flip the fish and sear on the other side.

6. When the fish is done, put it in the bowl with the sauce, cover the bowl, and put it in the fridge. Chill for about an hour.

7. To serve, cut the fish into thin slices about 1/2-inch thick and use the remaining sauce for dipping.

Serves 2

Garlic Clams *with* Crusty Garlic Dipping Bread

This is that dish you always see when you drive up the coast and stop at those cool little seafood places. Whether it's a local seafood dive or an upscale restaurant, you can find a version of this recipe. It's always nice to warm up with a nice hot broth on those chilly days. If you're not a vampire and love garlic, this dish is perfect for you.

2 tablespoons extra virgin olive oil

10 cloves garlic, minced

2 cups white wine (use the one you're drinking)

1 cup Snow's all-natural clam juice

1/2 stick butter

2 pounds clams, in shell, scrubbed clean

1 bunch fresh parsley, chopped

THE MOVES

1. Heat the oil in a medium-large pot over medium heat. (Make sure it's big enough to hold all the ingredients.)

2. Add the garlic and sauté about 1 minute.

3. Add white wine and clam juice. Bring to a boil and cook until it reduces by half, (about 10 minutes).

4. Add butter to the pot. When the butter is melted, add the clams and cover.

5. Cook until most of the clams open. Not all will open. Throw away the ones that don't.

6. Transfer the clams and juice to 2 bowls, sprinkle the parsley around the clams. Serve with garlic bread.

Serves 2

 **4-1-1 TIPS**

* Littleneck and Cherrystone Clams work best.

* If you don't want to deal with whole clams and just want the awesome dipping sauce, you can use a can of Snow's all natural clams.

Barbecued Salmon *with* Ginger Maple Glaze

This is a funky recipe. Salmon and maple syrup go well together like teriyaki and chicken. The ginger adds a nice bite that contrasts the sweetness. If you're hesitant, I say, "Live a little."

{
1/4 cup maple syrup

1 tablespoon minced fresh ginger

1 pound salmon, de-boned

THE MOVES

1. Combine the ginger and maple syrup in a small saucepan, simmer over low heat until reduced to a thick sauce. Remove from heat and cool.

2. In a separate bowl large enough to fit the whole piece of salmon, combine the salmon and the reduction sauce. Rub the salmon with the sauce until covered it is evenly covered.

3. Fire up the grill and cook the salmon over medium heat for about 6 minutes on each side, basting with the glaze often.

Serves 2

✳ 4-1-1 TIP

If your piece of salmon has the skin on, cook the flesh side first.

Veggin' Out

IT SEEMS LIKE MORE AND MORE PEOPLE are becoming vegetarians or at least trying to eat more veggies. Nana always says to me, "Eat your roughage." She's 90, so it must be working. Don't be thrown off kilter if your date only eats veggies. All that means is that she's probably going to outlive you. You can still eat veggies and not be a vegetarian; it just means you're a smart-a-tarian.

These veggie side dishes can be paired with any of my entrée recipes to create a complete meal for a fantastic date night.

WHAT'S HOT? • *Not dying of a massive coronary* • *Sweet potatoes* • *Anything fungi*

Winter Veggie Melt

When that flu season kicks in and your body is screaming for nutrition, try this simple and healthy melt to get you through the rest of the day.

2 tablespoons honey mustard

2 6-inch whole wheat sandwich rolls

4 tomato slices

5 mushrooms, sliced thin

4 red onion slices

1 zucchini, sliced thin

1 bunch alfalfa sprouts

4 thin slices Swiss cheese

THE MOVES

1. Cut each roll in half if they are not already halved. Spread mustard on two of the halves.

2. On top of the mustard layer 2 of the tomato slices, half of the mushrooms, 2 onion slices, half of the zucchini, half of the sprouts, and 2 slices of the cheese.

3. Put all four of the pieces of the rolls in a toaster oven and toast until cheese is melted and bread is a golden crispy brown. Remove from the oven, combine the rolls to make a sandwich, and serve.

Serves 2

Grilled Tomatoes

How simple and delectable is this? If your date loves tomatoes, you won't miss with this recipe.

{
2 tomatoes, cut in half   2 cloves garlic, minced

1 tablespoon olive oil   Pinch sea salt

1 teaspoon dried basil   1/3 cup Parmesan cheese

THE MOVES

1. Preheat a grill to 350 degrees F (medium heat).

2. In a small bowl combine the oil, basil, garlic, and sea salt.

3. Grill the tomatoes cut side down for 5 minutes. Flip the tomatoes.

4. Pour the oil mixture over the top of the tomatoes and cook for another 5 minutes or until they are soft and tender.

5. Sprinkle the Parmesan cheese on the tomatoes and serve.

Serves 2-4

Butter and Cinnamon Mashed Sweet Potatoes

Since sweet potatoes are really popular, here's a twist using them for mashed potatoes.

{
2 sweet potatoes

1 teaspoon cinnamon

2 tablespoons butter

THE MOVES

1. Bake sweet potatoes in the oven or toaster oven at 350 degrees F for 20 minutes or until tender. When cool enough to touch, peel off the skin.

2. Mash the potatoes in a large bowl until smooth.

3. Add the cinnamon and butter and mix well.

Serves 2

Steamed Asparagus

Any type of veggie steamed is a great accompaniment to a meal, but asparagus is also an aphrodisiac, so that's the one I would choose.

1 bunch asparagus

THE MOVES

1. Rinse under cold water and snap off the woody ends of each stalk.

2. Place in a steaming basket over boiling water. Steam for approximately five minutes, or until the asparagus is al dente.

3. Transfer to a serving platter and drizzle one of the dressings (below) over the asparagus.

Serves 2

Drizzle Effect Dressing

1/4 stick butter

1 teaspoon soy sauce

1 teaspoon balsamic vinegar

THE MOVES

1. Heat a small saucepan over medium heat.

2. Add all three ingredients to the saucepan and stir continuously until thickened, about 5 minutes.

Serves 2

Parsley Lemon Juice Dressing

{
2 cloves garlic, minced

Juice of 1 lemon

1 teaspoon red wine vinegar

1 teaspoon olive oil

Pepper to taste

THE MOVE

1. Combine all ingredients and mix until well blended.

Serves 2

Pan Steamed Tofu

Tofu is like a sponge and will absorb all the flavors you add to it. But first you need to drain the excess water from it by wrapping it in a paper towel and pressing down on it. This will also help it hold together better while being cooked.

{
1 cup water or vegetable broth

1 tablespoon soy sauce

1 piece ginger (quarter-size), peeled and minced

1 tablespoon rice vinegar

1 teaspoon sesame oil

2-5 cloves garlic, minced

1 green onion, chopped

1 pound firm tofu

THE MOVES

1. Heat a medium skillet over medium heat and add all the ingredients except the tofu. Bring to a boil while stirring.

2. Add the tofu and cover. Cook for about 3 minutes and then flip the tofu over. Cook for another 3 minutes.

3. Remove the tofu from the skillet, cut it in half lengthwise and then in half again, and serve.

Serves 2

Green Beans and Mushrooms in Garlic Sauce

There's something mysterious about why mushrooms, green beans, and garlic are so flavorful together. When my nose got a hit of the fragrant smell, I wondered to myself, can I bottle this stuff and wear it?

{
2 tablespoons extra virgin olive oil

3-6 cloves garlic, minced

2 cups fresh green beans, washed and both ends cut off

2 cups mushrooms, cut into quarters (button, baby browns, or portobello)

THE MOVES

1. Heat oil in a medium skillet over medium heat.

2. Add garlic and sauté for about 1 minute.

3. Add green beans and mushrooms and sauté for about 5 minutes or until mushrooms start to brown and the green beans are al dente.

Serves 2-4

Roasted Onions *with* Rosemary

You're going to need foil for this one. I serve this with a baked potato, and it's a combo made in vegetable heaven. The onion turns sweet and caramelizes when cooked releasing all of its lovable flavors.

{

2 medium onions, peeled

2 teaspoons olive oil

2 sprigs rosemary, chopped

2 cloves garlic, minced

Salt and pepper to taste

THE MOVES

1. Preheat oven to 400 degrees F.

2. Mix together the oil, rosemary, garlic, salt, and pepper. Coat the onions with the oil mixture.

3. Wrap the onions in two separate squares of foil so they are both completely sealed and cannot leak.

4. Bake for 30-45 minutes or until soft and tender when pierced with a knife.

5. Remove onions from the foil, slice, and serve.

Serves 2

 4-1-1 TIPS

* The hip onions to use are: sweet Maui onions and Mayan onions.

* There is a trick to cutting onions that will ensure that you don't look like a cry baby in front of your date: put a small piece of bread in your mouth. No joke—it really works.

Pajama Yammies

These were my favorite as a kid, and anyone who loves yams will love this recipe.

{
2 yams, washed, peeled, and cut into quarters

1 teaspoon orange zest

3/4 cup orange juice

1 tablespoon honey

THE MOVES

1. Preheat oven to 350 degrees F.

2. Boil the yams in a medium pot of boiling water until tender, about 5 minutes.

3. Drain yams and transfer to an ovenproof dish.

4. In a small bowl, combine the zest, orange juice, and honey. Mix well.

5. Put the yams in a baking dish and pour the orange mixture over them. Bake for 10 minutes.

Serves 2

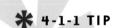 **4-1-1 TIP**

Nuts, raisins, marshmallows, or coconut pieces can be added to this dish, or go big and add them all!

Creamed Spinach

Here's my healthy twist to this old-school dish. I'm just not a big believer in using a lot of cream because it always makes me feel bloated and full...and I'm a guy! So I use milk.

{
1/4 stick butter

1 small onion, chopped

2-5 cloves garlic, minced

3 tablespoons all purpose flour

1 1/2 cups milk

1 10-ounce package frozen spinach, thawed and drained

Salt and pepper to taste

THE MOVES

1. Heat butter in a large saucepan over medium heat. Add onion and garlic. Sauté for about 5 minutes.

2. Add flour and whisk until smooth and then gradually stir in milk, stirring constantly with a wooden spoon until sauce thickens and starts to boil. Simmer for about 1 minute.

3. Add spinach, salt, and pepper to taste. Stir until spinach is completely incorporated in the sauce.

4. Turn down the heat and cook for another 5 minutes.

Serves 2-4

✳ 4-1-1 TIPS

* To drain thawed spinach, squeeze out the excess liquid with your fingers.
* If you prefer fresh spinach, you'll need 2 bunches. Fresh spinach needs to be cleaned really well because it will have dirt in and around it. Cut off the stems just leaving the leaves and roughly chop.

Foil Steamed Zucchini

If you were lucky like me and grew up where all your family could grow was zucchini, this one is for you. If you're feeling nostalgic or you actually just like zucchini, try this super simple recipe.

{
1 10x10-inch piece of foil

1 medium-large zucchini, chopped

1 teaspoon butter

1 teaspoon sea salt

2 tablespoons water

1 teaspoon Parmesan cheese

THE MOVES

1. Preheat oven or toaster oven to 350 degrees F.

2. Fold foil to make a pouch.

3. Add zucchini, butter, sea salt, and water. Seal up the foil securely around all edges.

4. Place in the oven and bake for 10 minutes or until zucchini is tender but not soggy.

5. Put in a serving bowl and sprinkle with the Parmesan cheese.

Serves 1-2

Vegetable Stir Fry *with* Mustard, Ginger, and Soy Sauce

You don't need a wok to stir fry; you can use a semi-deep skillet. The trick is to actually stir the ingredients while they are pan-frying. Hence, stir fry. You can add tofu or chicken for a protein kick.

{
2 tablespoons vegetable oil

2 cups (total) cauliflower, baby carrots, and broccoli, diced

1/2 cup snow peas

1 8-ounce can water chestnuts, drained

3 tablespoons Chinese mustard

1 tablespoon grated fresh ginger

1/4 cup low sodium soy sauce

Juice of 1/2 lemon

Pepper to taste

THE MOVES

1. Heat the oil in a medium deep skillet over medium high heat.

2. Add all of the veggies and sauté for about 3-5 minutes, stirring continuously.

3. In a medium bowl combine the mustard, ginger, soy sauce, lemon juice, and pepper.

4. Add the sauce to the veggies in the skillet and stir fry for another 5-7 minutes or until veggies are fork tender.

Serves 2

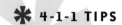

✳ 4-1-1 TIPS

* If you like your veggies al dente, reduce stir-fry time by a couple of minutes.

* You don't need to add salt because the soy sauce covers that. Even the low sodium has a good amount of salt.

Double Stuffed Baked Potato

Americans love potatoes, and this recipe is my attempt to get people to eat more of them that are not deep-fried. I promise that this recipe is tastier than French fries.

{
2 russet potatoes, washed and dried

2 cloves garlic, minced

1/2 cup milk

1/2 stick butter

1/2 cup shredded Cheddar cheese

Salt and pepper to taste

THE MOVES

1. Preheat the oven to 450 degrees F.

2. Wash the potatoes well, pierce several times with a fork, and then bake for about 45 minutes or until they are soft enough to pierce with a knife. Remove from the oven and cool. Keep the oven set at 450 degrees F.

3. When cool enough to touch, cut a diamond shaped section from the top of each potato, peel back the skin and discard.

4. With a spoon, carve out the inner potato (leaving skin shell intact) and place in a medium bowl.

5. To the bowl add garlic, milk, butter, half of the cheese, salt, and pepper. Mix until blended well or until your hand falls off, whichever comes first.

6. Stuff the potato mixture back into the potato skin shell and then top with the remaining cheese.

7. Transfer the potatoes to a shallow baking dish and put them back in the oven to bake for another 10 minutes or until cheese is nice and melted.

Serves 2

WHAT'S HOT? *VINO!* • *Anything Italian* • *Homemade sauces*

Passionate Pastas

PASTA IS THE COMFORT FOOD for the world, and nothing says *Viva Italia* like pasta does. Its popularity has maintained over the centuries because of its long shelf life and nutritional value.

There are more than 350 shapes of dried pasta in Italy known as Pasta Secca. If you like dried pasta, make sure you buy pasta made in Italy because, by Italian law, dried pasta must be made with 100 percent durum semolina flour and water. Making fresh pasta takes a great deal of care, and really one kind isn't better than any other— they are used for different situations and recipes. So take your pick and enjoy some very tasty and passionate pastas.

Make-out Macaroni *with* Lobster and Cheese Blend

When you make this recipe you're guaranteed to whet your date's whistle and get some serious kissing in. The real lobster and this delicious blend of cheeses make this an irresistible dish.

1 pound Barilla elbow macaroni

6 cups water

3 tablespoons butter

3 tablespoons all purpose flour

1 tablespoon mustard

2 cups milk

1 small yellow onion, finely chopped

1/2 teaspoon paprika

Salt and pepper to taste

1-2 pounds cooked lobster tail, coarsely chopped

3 cups (total) of the following mix of cheeses:

Parmesan, grated

Romano, grated

Sharp Cheddar, shredded

Mozzarella, shredded

Gouda, shredded

Pepper Jack, shredded

Breadcrumb Topping :

3 tablespoons butter

1 cup panko breadcrumbs

THE MOVES

1. Preheat oven to 350 degrees F.

2. Add the water to a large pot and bring to a boil. Cook the macaroni al dente. Drain and set aside.

3. In another pot over medium heat melt the butter. Stir in flour and mustard. Keep stirring until there are no lumps.

4. Add milk, onion, paprika, salt, pepper, and 2 1/4 cups of the cheese combination. Stir well. Turn heat to low and simmer for 10 minutes.

5. Add macaroni to cheese sauce and mix well.

6. Add lobster meat and mix well.

7. Transfer to an 8x10-inch baking dish or casserole dish.

8. Top with the remaining cheese.

9. In a small saucepan over medium heat melt butter. Add breadcrumbs and mix.

10. Spread the breadcrumb topping evenly over the macaroni.

11. Bake for 30 minutes or until the cheese is bubbling and golden brown.

Serves 6-8

Nudees (or Gnudi)

I like being a nudee, and you'll love this hot new pasta-style dumpling similar to gnocchi or a croquette. Basically this is the filling in ravioli. The trick is to use fresh ricotta cheese. You also want to use a simple but flavorful sauce, so take a look at the simple sauces in this chapter, and use any one of those.

2 cups ricotta cheese

1 bunch fresh spinach

1/4 cup Parmesan or Romano cheese

3 eggs

1/2 teaspoon nutmeg

Salt and pepper to taste

1 cup all purpose flour

THE MOVES

1. Place the ricotta cheese in a bowl lined with paper towels and drain for at least 30 minutes.

2. Wash the spinach well and then boil in a small amount of water for 5 minutes. Pour in a colander and squeeze out excess water. Remove the stems and finely chop.

3. In a large bowl combine ricotta, spinach, cheese, and eggs. Mix well.

4. Add the nutmeg, salt, pepper, and 5 tablespoons of the flour. Mix well.

5. Make nuclear-size nudees by rolling 2 tablespoons of the mixture into balls.

6. Dredge the nudees in remaining flour to coat, tapping off any excess.

7. Bring a medium-large pot of salted water to a boil.

8. Drop nudees in boiling water and cook for about 5 minutes or until they float to the top.

9. Scoop out the nudees with a slotted spoon.

10. Arrange on a plate and drizzle with one of my simple pasta sauces.

Serves 2

Veggie Lasagna Rolls

This is the hot new twist on traditional lasagna. Each roll is like an individual, personalized piece of lasagna.

10 lasagna noodles

1 egg

1 pound ricotta

1 1/2 cups fresh mozzarella

1/2 cup Parmesan

**1 cup veggies, finely chopped
(spinach, mushrooms, zucchini, broccoli, tomatoes)**

1/4 cup chopped fresh parsley

Garlic salt and pepper to taste

2 cups tomato sauce

THE MOVES

1. Cook lasagna noodles according to package directions. Drain.

2. Preheat oven to 350 degrees F.

3. In a large bowl combine egg, ricotta, half of the mozzarella, Parmesan, veggies, parsley, garlic salt, and pepper. Mix well.

4. Spread the noodles out on a cutting board. Spread a thin layer of the veggie mixture evenly over each noodle.

5. Starting at one end, roll up each noodle.

6. In a shallow baking dish spread 1 cup of the tomato sauce on the bottom.

7. Add the rolls, seam side down, so they don't unroll and fall apart.

8. Add remaining tomato sauce and remaining mozzarella cheese on top of rolls.

9. Bake for 30-40 minutes or until cooked through and cheese is melted.

Serves 2

Shrimp and Garlic Linguini *with* White Wine Sauce

This is a nice and light sauce that won't make you feel full and heavy. Use whatever white wine you are drinking for the sauce, which means you might have to get 2 bottles. Bummer!

2 tablespoons extra virgin olive oil

5 cloves garlic, minced

1 pound medium-size uncooked shrimp, shells removed, cleaned and de-veined

Salt and pepper to taste

1 cup white wine

1 pound linguini

2 tablespoons chopped fresh parsley

1 cup Parmesan cheese

THE MOVES

1. Heat oil in a large skillet over medium high heat. Add garlic and sauté for 2 minutes.

2. Add shrimp, salt, and pepper. Stir together.

3. Add wine and bring to a boil. Reduce heat and simmer for 10 minutes.

4. In a separate pot boil linguini until al dente. Drain and add to sauce, folding pasta in until fully mixed.

5. Transfer to a pasta serving bowl and sprinkle with parsley.

6. Put the Parmesan cheese in a shallow bowl with a spoon so your date can add it at will.

Serves 2

✳ 4-1-1 TIPS

* Pinot Grigio works well in this recipe. If you want a more buttery, earthy flavor use Chardonnay.

* Break the linguini in half so the pieces aren't so long. This will prevent you from having to slurp up your pasta, which while on a date is not recommended.

Light Lasagna *with* Cottage Cheese

This is the traditional way of making lasagna. My mom worked in Italian restaurants and used to make this for us all the time. Her trick is to use cottage cheese so it's lighter and not as cheesy. I know what you're saying: "It's too hard, and it takes to long." Now that you're older and don't live with your mother, go to the store, buy the ingredients, and get to work. Your date will love it!

9 lasagna noodles

1 1/2 cups cottage cheese

1 egg, whisked

1/2 cup grated Parmesan cheese

Salt and Pepper to taste

3 cups tomato sauce

12 ounces grated mozzarella cheese

THE MOVES

1. Preheat oven to 375 degrees F.

2. Prepare noodles as instructed on package and drain.

3. In a medium bowl combine cottage cheese, egg, Parmesan, salt, and pepper.

4. Spread 1 cup of the tomato sauce across the bottom of a medium baking dish. Lay 3 noodles down in the baking dish and cover with half of the cheese mixture. Sprinkle with mozzarella and top with tomato sauce.

5. Repeat procedure for one more layer ending with the last three noodles and then sauce. Top with remaining mozzarella.

6. Bake for 35-45 minutes or until sauce is bubbling. Remove from oven and let lasagna stand for 10 minutes or you'll burn your mouth off.

Serves 2

4-1-1 TIP

You can turn this into a meat lasagna by adding cooked ground beef or turkey to the tomato sauce.

SIMPLE SAUCES FOR EVERYDAY PASTAS

You can make these ahead and save the sauce in plastic storage containers, as they will stay good for a week. The longer these sauces sit the more the flavors fuse together.

Aunt Val's Simple and Spicy Spaghetti Sauce

This is my family's go-to spaghetti sauce. My aunt and my nana would make this, and they like their sauce with a little bite to it. So if you like it spicy, this is the sauce for you.

1 tablespoon olive oil

2 small onions, chopped

5 cloves garlic, chopped

2 cups tomato juice

1 cup tomato puree

1 6-ounce can tomato paste

4 hot yellow chiles, left whole or chopped

1 can olives with pimientos

Salt and Pepper to taste

1 pound ground beef

THE MOVES

1. Heat a large pot over medium heat and add oil, onion, and garlic. Sauté for about 3-5 minutes.

2. Add tomato juice, tomato puree, tomato paste, chiles, olives, salt, and pepper. Mix well.

3. Add ground beef and bring to a boil, then reduce heat and cover. Simmer for at least 30 minutes.

4. Serve over your favorite pasta and add a sprinkle of Parmesan or Romano cheese.

Serves 2

APHRODISIAC #12: Asparagus

Given its suggestive phallic shape, asparagus is frequently enjoyed as an aphrodisiac food. It happens to be high in vitamin E, considered one of the sex hormone stimulants.

APHRODISIAC #13: Basil

It is believed that basil stimulates the sex drive, boosts fertility, and produces a general sense of well being for body and mind.

APHRODISIAC #14: Vanilla

The scent and flavor of vanilla is believed to increase lust.

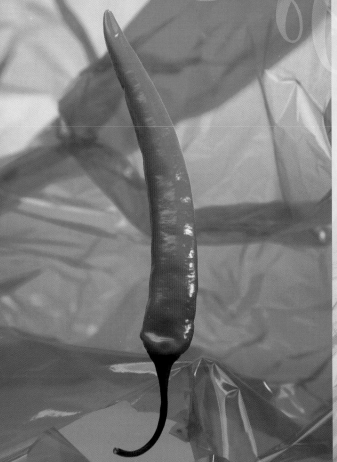

APHRODISIAC #15: Chiles

Capsaicin, which is found in chiles and curries, stimulates nerve endings to release chemicals, raising the heart rate and triggering the release of endorphins that create a pleasurable feeling of a natural high. Capsaicin is also what gives chiles and curries their heat.

APHRODISIAC #16: Oysters

Documented as an aphrodisiac food by the Romans and considered the food of love, legend has it that Casanova ate dozens of oysters every day. The truth is that oysters are high in zinc, a mineral used in the production of testosterone and protein.

Walnut Sauce

{

2 slices white bread

1 cup milk

1/2 cup walnuts, shelled

2 cloves garlic, whole

Pinch of salt

3 tablespoons olive oil

THE MOVES

1. Remove crusts from the bread. Soak the bread in a little milk, just enough to wet the bread, for 5 minutes.

2. Put the bread in a blender or food processor. Add the walnuts, garlic, and salt. Blend until all ingredients are well combined.

3. Add the olive oil and blend again. If the sauce seems too thick, thin with a little milk.

4. Serve over your favorite pasta.

Serves 2

Butter and Sage Sauce

This simple sauce has a nice earthy flavor. The trick is to brown the butter.

{

1 stick butter

10 fresh sage leaves, chopped

THE MOVES

1. Melt butter in a small saucepan over medium heat.

2. Add sage and cook until it is crispy and the butter is browned, stirring frequently to avoid burning the butter.

3. Serve over your favorite pasta

Serves 2

Turkey Ragu

This recipe is nice and thick and will work with any pasta. Serve with a rustic-style garlic bread. In fact, you really don't even need pasta for this dish; just dunk your bread in the thick juicy sauce and enjoy!

1 tablespoon extra virgin olive oil

3-5 cloves garlic, minced

1 small yellow onion, chopped

1 pound ground turkey

1 8-ounce can tomato paste

5 Roma tomatoes, chopped

1 tablespoon Italian herb mix

Salt and pepper to taste

1 cup water

THE MOVES

1. Heat the oil in a large skillet over medium heat. Add garlic and onion. Sauté for about 3-5 minutes.

2. Add the turkey, tomato paste, tomatoes, herbs, salt, and pepper. Mix together until well blended.

3. Add water and bring to a boil. Reduce the heat and simmer for at least 30 minutes (the longer, the better).

4. Serve over your favorite pasta.

Serves 2

Simple White Sauce

2 tablespoons butter

2 tablespoons flour

Pinch of salt and pepper

1 cup milk

THE MOVES

1. Melt butter in a small saucepan over medium heat. Add flour and stir until smooth.

2. Add salt, pepper, and milk.

3. Cover and cook until the sauce is thick and bubbly, stirring occasionally.

4. Serve over your favorite pasta.

Serves 2

Sexy Sauces

AS THE SAYING GOES, it's all about the sex—I mean the sauce.
This section is all about making homespun and creative sauces because
creativity = sexitivity.

These sauces are some of my favorites from around the world,
and I've included suggestions as to what foods they go best with.

Spicy Rooster Sauce

Great with Asian dishes and as a marinade.

> 1/2 stick butter
>
> 2 cloves garlic, minced
>
> 1 green onion, chopped
>
> 1 cup chicken broth
>
> 1/4 cup soy sauce
>
> 1 tablespoon Sriracha chili sauce (a.k.a. rooster sauce)

THE MOVES

1. In a saucepan over medium heat add butter, garlic, and green onion. Sauté for 3 minutes.

2. Add chicken broth, soy sauce, and Sriracha sauce.

3. Bring to a boil then reduce heat and simmer. The sauce is done when it has reduced by half.
   (For marinade: Just mix all the ingredients together without heating and marinate chicken, pork, or beef for 30-60 minutes.)

Serves 2

Red Wine Sage Sauce

Great with steak.

{
1 tablespoon butter

1 shallot, peeled and finely chopped

Salt and pepper to taste

1/2 cup red wine

3 tablespoons finely chopped fresh sage

THE MOVES

1. In a saucepan over medium heat add butter and shallot. Sauté for 2-3 minutes.

2. Add salt, pepper, and red wine. Bring to a boil, then reduce heat and simmer until reduced by half.

3. Add sage and mix well.

Serves 2

Mustard Vinaigrette

Great with salads and chicken.

{
2 tablespoons mustard

1 tablespoon balsamic vinegar

2 tablespoons extra virgin olive oil

THE MOVES

1. In a bowl combine the mustard and balsamic vinegar.

2. Whisk in the olive oil very slowly. Keep whisking until blended.

Serves 2

Hot Pink Vodka Sauce

Great with fish and pasta.

{
1 tablespoon extra virgin olive oil

1 tablespoon butter

2 cloves garlic, minced

2 shallots, peeled and minced

1 cup vodka (use your favorite)

1 cup chicken broth

1 32-ounce can crushed tomatoes

Salt and pepper to taste

1/2 cup heavy cream

10 leaves fresh basil, washed and chopped

THE MOVES

1. In a large saucepan over medium heat add oil, butter, garlic, and shallots. Sauté for 3 to 5 minutes until they sweat (hopefully not like your date).

2. Add vodka to the pan and cook until reduced by half, about 4-5 minutes.

3. Add chicken broth, tomatoes, salt, and pepper. Bring to a boil. Reduce heat and simmer.

4. Add cream, stirring well. Bring back to a boil. Once the sauce has boiled, it is done.

Serves 2

Pesto Sauce

Great with pastas, as a spread on sandwiches or bagels, and as a bread dipping sauce.

- **2 cups fresh basil**
- **1 cup fresh parsley**
- **1/2 cup grated Parmesan or Romano cheese**
- **1/2 cup toasted pine nuts**
- **4 cloves garlic, peeled and roughly chopped**
- **1/4 teaspoon salt**
- **1/2 cup olive oil**
- **1 tablespoon lemon juice**
- **2 tablespoons water**

THE MOVE

1. Combine all ingredients in a food processor or blender. Puree until the mixture forms a smooth, thick paste.

Serves2

White Wine and Butter Sauce

Great with white fish and as a dipping sauce for shellfish.
This sauce is also known as beurre blanc.

- **1/2 stick butter**
- **2 cloves garlic, minced**
- **1/2 cup white wine**
- **1/2 teaspoon Old Bay seasoning**

THE MOVES

1. In a small saucepan over low heat add butter, garlic, white wine, and seasoning.
2. Simmer for at least 10 minutes.

Serves 2

Champagne Sauce

Great with oysters and clams.

{
- **1 cup champagne**
- **2 cups heavy cream**
- **1/4 cup melted butter**

THE MOVES

1. In a medium saucepan over medium heat reduce the champagne by half.
2. Add the cream and cook until reduced by half.
3. Add butter and stir until the sauce thickens.

Serves 4

Black Cherry Sauce

Great with game meats, like duck, quail, venison, and boar.

{
- **1 8-ounce jar black cherry jam**
- **1/2 cup chili sauce**
- **1/2 cup beef broth**
- **1/2 teaspoon Dijon mustard**

THE MOVE

1. In a medium saucepan over medium heat add jam, chili sauce, broth, and mustard. Bring to a boil and then simmer for 20 minutes.

Serves 4

Ginger Citrus Soy Sauce

Great with fish and salads.

{
1 tablespoon olive oil

1/2 cup thinly sliced ginger

2 shallots, peeled and thinly sliced

5 cloves garlic, peeled and sliced

1 cup white wine

2 tablespoons soy sauce

1 cup grapefruit juice

1 cup orange juice

Juice of 1 lemon

THE MOVES

1. In a medium saucepan over medium heat add the oil and ginger and sauté for 2-3 minutes.

2. Add shallots and garlic and sauté for another 2 minutes.

3. Add wine, soy sauce, grapefruit juice, orange juice, and lemon juice.

4. Bring to a boil, reduce heat and simmer until reduced by half.

Serves 4

Blood Orange Sauce

Great with pork and chicken.

{
Juice of 6 blood oranges

Juice of 2 lemons

2 tablespoons sugar

1 cup port

1/2 stick butter

THE MOVES

1. In a small saucepan over medium high heat, add the orange juice, lemon juice, sugar, port, and butter. Stir and bring to a boil.

2. Simmer until reduced by half.

Serves 4

Roasted Garlic, Rosemary and Butter Sauce

Great with steak.

{
3 bulbs garlic, roasted

1 tablespoon olive oil

3 sprigs rosemary leaves

1 cup chicken broth

1 stick butter

THE MOVES

1. Preheat oven to 400 degrees F.

2. To roast the garlic bulbs, first cut the tops off and rub the exposed ends of each bulb with a small amount of olive oil. Wrap each bulb separately in foil and bake at 400 degrees F for 30 minutes.

3. Remove the roasted bulbs from the foil and squeeze out the soft garlic cloves.

4. In a small saucepan over medium heat add the garlic cloves, rosemary, broth, and butter. Blend until butter is melted.

Serves 2

Guilty Pleasures

WOMEN LOVE CHOCOLATE and guys love anything sweet and juicy. In a sense, these recipes are a little forbidden because they are so sexy and tasty. Try some of these mouthwatering treats to finish off a perfect meal.

WHAT'S HOT? • *Dark Chocolate* • *Marzipan* • *Mangoes*

Vanilla Roasted Mango *with* Mango Sorbet

Need I say more (than the recipe name) about these flavors fusing together harmoniously?
The blending of these flavors is just like you and your date sharing this tasty treat.

- 4 tablespoons butter
- 1/4 cup brown sugar
- 1 vanilla bean, split lengthwise
- 2-4 mangoes, peeled and sliced
- 1/2 cup water
- 4 scoops mango sorbet

THE MOVES

1. Preheat oven to 375 degrees F.

2. In an ovenproof pan over medium heat melt the butter.

3. Add the brown sugar and vanilla bean. Stir until the sugar is melted and caramelized, 3 to 5 minutes.

4. Add the mango to the pan and simmer for about a minute.

5. Add the water to the pan, cover, and transfer it to the oven. Roast for about 10 minutes.

6. When ready to serve, remove the vanilla bean and assemble the dessert: In tall glasses, place a scoop of the sorbet then the warm mango. Drizzle with the juices from the pan. Repeat the layers to the top of the glass and serve immediately.

Serves 2

4-1-1 TIP
OXO makes a mango slicer/de-seeder that is super simple to use without making a big mess.

The Ultimate Dude Dessert
(a.k.a. Cherry Heaven)

I must admit, this is a must-have for guys who like cherry desserts and cherry flavored beer at the same time. I like to call it going to cherry heaven.

2 pieces of cherry pie, fresh and hot

2 scoops Ben & Jerry's Cherry Garcia ice cream

1 pint Lindemans Kriek Belgium beer

THE MOVES

1. Place pie slices on two separate plates.
2. Place a scoop of ice cream on each piece of pie.
3. Pour 1 cup of the beer over each or serve separately in a beer mug.

Serves 2

The Ultimate Chick Dessert
(a.k.a. Homemade Cookie Sandwich with Melted Chocolate)

I was at a restaurant once and saw a waiter carry this monstrosity of a cookie to a really cute gal. That inspired me to go home and create my own. Here's what I came up with. I am a big fan of Ben & Jerry's, but you can use any ice cream you like.

1 package dark chocolate chip Toll House cookie dough

1 bar chocolate, melted

2 big scoops Ben & Jerry's vanilla ice cream

THE MOVES

1. Using the cookie dough make four large cookies (5-6 inches in diameter). Bake according to package directions.
2. While the cookies are baking, heat a small saucepan over medium heat and melt the chocolate bar.
3. Once the cookies are baked and while they are still warm, place a scoop of ice cream on two of the cookies.
4. Drizzle the melted chocolate over the ice cream and put the remaining cookies on top to complete the cookie sandwiches. Serve immediately.

Serves 2

Dark Strawberries of Love

I've made this recipe so many times, and it is always a great hit. I like to make extra because my neighbors come by and then the strawberries mysteriously disappear.

{
1 12x12-inch piece of wax paper

1 bar dark chocolate

10 strawberries, washed and dried

THE MOVES

1. Lay the piece of wax paper on the counter.

2. In a pot over low heat melt the chocolate bar, stirring constantly until creamy.

3. Dip the strawberries, one at a time, in the chocolate turning and covering until half of the strawberry is coated. Place the strawberries on wax paper and chill in the refrigerator until you are ready to serve.

Serves 2

Red Wine Poached Pears

Talk about fancy-schmancy. If you pull off this dessert you're going to be a big hit.

{
2 cups red wine	**2 cloves**
1 cup sugar	**1 orange, sliced thin**
1/2 stick cinnamon	**2 pears, peeled and stem left on**

THE MOVES

1. In a large pot combine wine, sugar, cinnamon, cloves, and orange slices. Stir until sugar is dissolved and then place on the stove over medium low heat and bring to a simmer.

2. Add pears to the pot and simmer for 30-60 minutes or until the pears are tender but not mushy. Place a small plate on the pears to keep them from floating.

3. Carefully remove the pears using a slotted spoon and put each on a separate plate with remaining sauce drizzled around the plate.

Serves 2

Pine Nut Cookies

This is a nice twist to the usual cookie. This is a good dessert to choose if your overall meal also included pine nuts.

{
1 stick plus 1 tablespoon unsalted butter, room temperature

1/2 cup sugar

1 teaspoon vanilla extract

1 teaspoon ground fennel seed

1/4 teaspoon salt

1 large egg

1 cup all purpose flour

1/4 cup pine nuts

THE MOVES

1. In a large bowl using an electric mixer beat the butter, sugar, vanilla, fennel seed, and salt until light and fluffy.

2. Add the egg and blend until combined.

3. Add the flour and mix just until blended.

4. Add pine nuts and mix just until blended.

5. Lightly dust a clean surface with flour and roll out the dough. Shape into a 10-inch log.

6. Cut 1/4-inch thick rounds from the dough log. Refrigerate for about 2 hours.

7. Preheat the oven to 350 degrees F.

8. Grease a baking sheet and space cookies two inches apart.

9. Bake until the cookies are golden around the edges, about 15 minutes.

Serves 6

Banana Bread *with* Warm Banana Maple Syrup

If you like bananas, this is the recipe for you. Make this dessert for your date and see if she likes them, too. This could make or break the proverbial banana leaf. Just a heads-up, you'll need 3 bowls and a 9 x 5 x 3-inch loaf pan to make this recipe right.

{

1 cup sugar

1 stick butter, room temperature

2 large eggs

3 bananas, soft and ripe

1 tablespoon milk

1 teaspoon ground cinnamon

2 cups all purpose flour

1 teaspoon baking powder

1 teaspoon baking soda

1 teaspoon salt

1 cup maple syrup

THE MOVES

1. Preheat the oven to 325 degrees F.

2. In a bowl using an electric mixer beat the sugar and 6 tablespoons of the butter until light and fluffy. Add the eggs one at a time and mix well.

3. Peel the bananas and in another bowl mash 2 of the bananas with a fork. Add the milk and cinnamon and stir.

4. In a third bowl combine the flour, baking powder, baking soda, and salt.

5. Add the banana mixture to the butter mixture and mix well. Then add the flour mixture and mix well.

6. Butter a 9 x 5 x 3-inch loaf pan.8. Pour batter into pan and bake for 1 hour or until a toothpick inserted in the center comes out clean.

7. Set aside to cool for about 15 minutes. Remove bread from pan and let cool completely before slicing.

For the Sauce:

1. In a skillet over medium high heat the remaining 2 tablespoons of butter.

2. Slice the remaining banana, add to the butter and cook for about 3 minutes, or until lightly browned.

3. Add maple syrup, mixing well. Bring to boiling and boil for 2 to 3 minutes, until the mixture is slightly thickened.

4. Serve the sauce warm over the sliced bread.

Serves 6

Picnics, Parties,

Movies, *and* Toasts

Peaceful Picnics

ARE YOU STRESSED? Are you overworked and underpaid? Or are you just tired of bad drivers and catching every red light trying to get home? This is the perfect excuse to pack up the picnic basket or cooler and disappear for the day. Find a trail, park, beach, river, or even your own backyard. It's all about relaxing and enjoying each other for a few hours. Don't forget the picnic blanket and wine bottle opener. The Liquid Love section on page 158 has cool ideas for drinks that you can take on your picnic.

WHAT'S HOT? • *Picnic baskets* • *Peace and quiet*
• *Finding a place away from prying eyes*

Creamy Chicken Salad

This recipe is cool and refreshing and can also be used as a dip, in a sandwich, or as a spread on crackers.

> **2 6.5-ounce cans chicken, in water**
> **1/4 cup Marie's blue cheese dressing**
> **1 stalk celery, finely chopped**
> **1 yellow bell pepper, finely chopped**
> **1 tablespoon Dijon mustard**
> **Salt and pepper to taste**

THE MOVES

1. Combine the chicken, dressing, celery, pepper, mustard, salt, and bell pepper in a medium bowl.
2. Stir until well mixed.
3. Transfer to a sealable bowl or plastic container. Chill in the fridge until ready to serve.

Serves 2

Pork Loin Sandwiches

This pork is also tasty by itself and fun to snack on when cut up in small pieces.

{
- 1 1-pound pork loin
- 1/4 cup lemon juice
- 1/4 cup lime juice
- 1/4 cup brown sugar
- 1/4 cup Worcestershire sauce
- 1/4 cup dry mustard
- 2-5 cloves garlic, chopped

- 1 tablespoon paprika
- Salt and pepper to taste
- 4 slices bread (your favorite)
- 1 tablespoon French's yellow mustard
- 4 tomato slices
- 4 leaves iceberg lettuce, washed and dried

THE MOVES

1. In a large re-sealable plastic bag add the pork loin, lemon juice, lime juice, brown sugar, Worcestershire, dry mustard, garlic, and paprika. Marinate for at least 2 hours in the refrigerator (overnight is best).

2. Preheat oven or grill to 350 degrees F. Bake or grill the pork loin for 45-60 minutes or until it is cooked through. Let it rest out of the oven for 3-5 minutes.

3. Slice the pork loin into 1/4-1/2-inch slices.

4. Spread mustard on two slices of the bread, top with the desired number of pork slices, sliced tomato, and lettuce. Top with remaining slices of bread to complete the sammie.

Serves 2

Turkey and Brie Melt

I first made this sandwich when I was picnicking in Sedona, Arizona. The Brie cheese melts perfectly with the turkey giving it a warm, creamy bite. Wrap these sandwiches in foil while they are still hot to keep the cheese melted for your picnic.

{
4 slices sourdough bread

1 teaspoon butter

1/2 pound sliced turkey

4 thin wedges of Brie cheese

1 cup Russian dressing, for dipping sauce (see recipe below)

THE MOVES

1. Heat up that grill, toaster oven, or oven to 350 degrees F.
2. Butter 1 side of each bread slice and then put them buttered side down on a clean work surface.
3. Divide the turkey and cheese and stack on one piece of the bread.
4. Top with the second slice of bread, buttered side up.
5. Heat the sandwich on the grill or in the oven and cook until the bread is nicely browned and the cheese is melted, about 5 minutes.
6. Cut the sandwiches in half and wrap them in foil to keep them warm.

Russian Dressing

Combine equal amounts of mayonnaise, sweet pickle relish, and catsup and mix together.

Serves 2

※ 4-1-1 TIP

The rind of Brie cheese has live bacteria in it, so eat that, too. It's good for your immune system.

Summer Tostada

When you want something light but with big flavor, try this refreshing tostada.

{
4 tostada shells

1 15-ounce can refried beans

1 can julienne beets, drained

1 cup shredded iceberg lettuce

3/4 cup Italian dressing

1/2 cup Parmesan cheese

THE MOVES

1. Spread a thin layer of beans evenly over each tostada.

2. In a medium bowl combine beets, lettuce, dressing, and Parmesan cheese. Sprinkle over beans.

Serves 2

Original Cuban Sub

Cuba is a passionate country, and hopefully this sub will spark some passion during your picnic.

{
2 hero-style French bread rolls

4 tablespoons French's yellow mustard

4 dill pickle slices

4 slices Swiss cheese

6 slices Virginia ham

4 slices roast pork

THE MOVES

1. Slice open the rolls on the top, not the side.

2. Spread the mustard on both sides.

3. Add two of the pickle slices and two of the cheese slices.

4. Fold ham slices in half add on top of the cheese, then add the pork slices.

5. Close the subs and grill them until the bread is nice and toasty and the cheese is melted.

Serves 2

Three Bean Salad *with* Red Wine Vinaigrette

One bean, two bean, three bean salad. This is my manage a tois of salads.

1 15-ounce can kidney beans, drained and rinsed

1 15-ounce can garbanzo beans, drained and rinsed

1 10-ounce package frozen green beans, thawed

2 tablespoons red wine vinegar

2 tablespoons Dijon mustard

Salt and pepper to taste

4 tablespoons olive oil

THE MOVES

1. Combine the kidney beans, garbanzo beans, and green beans in a large bowl.

2. Combine the red wine vinegar, mustard, salt, and pepper. Mix well.

3. Whisk the oil into the vinegar mixture and pour over bean mixture. Stir until well mixed.

Serves 2-4

Sweet and Sassy Red Potato Salad

The trick with this potato salad is not adding mayonnaise. The sweet comes from the sweet mustard and the sassy comes from the Italian dressing.

2 pounds red potatoes, quartered, boiled, and chilled

1/2 cup French's Sweet and Zesty Mustard

1/2 cup Italian dressing

1 small red onion, finely chopped

2 celery stalks, chopped

1 tablespoon chopped fresh dill

Salt and pepper to taste

THE MOVES

1. In a large bowl combine potatoes, mustard, dressing, red onion, celery, dill, salt, and pepper.

2. Stir until potatoes are well coated.

Serves 4

Costa Rican Coleslaw

I've been to Costa Rica, and what a beautiful, loving country it is. The motto there is pura vida! It means pure life, which we all need to work on. So I highly recommend you take a trip there. Until then enjoy yourself wherever your picnic takes you.

1/2 head shredded green cabbage, or 3 cups

1/4 wedge shredded red cabbage

1/4 cup hot sauce

1/2 cup mayonnaise

Juice of 1/2 lime

1 teaspoon Frank's RedHot Chile 'n Lime Hot Sauce

Garlic salt and pepper to taste

1 tomato, chopped (optional)

THE MOVES

1. Combine green and red cabbage in a large bowl.

2. In a separate bowl combine the hot sauce, mayonnaise, lime juice, Frank's sauce, garlic salt, and pepper. Stir until well mixed.

3. Pour the sauce onto the cabbage and mix until well blended. Top with chopped tomato, if desired.

4. Chill in the fridge until you are ready to serve.

Serves 2

Cucumber, Tomato, and Onion Salad

What a cool and refreshing salad. My Man Spritzer drink (page 158) goes really well with this.

2 cucumbers, washed, peeled, and sliced thin

2 Roma tomatoes, washed and chopped

1 small red onion, peeled and sliced thin

1 teaspoon sesame seeds

1/2 cup rice wine vinegar

1 tablespoon French's mustard

Salt and pepper to taste

THE MOVES

1. Combine cucumbers, tomatoes, and onion in a sealable bowl or plastic container.

2. In a separate bowl combine sesame seeds, vinegar, mustard, salt, and pepper and mix well.

3. Pour the dressing over the cucumber mixture, secure the lid tightly, and shake until well mixed.

4. Chill in the fridge until ready to serve.

Serves 2

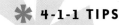

✳ 4-1-1 TIPS

The longer this marinates in the fridge the better it tastes.

Movie Night

SO YOU'VE DECIDED to enjoy each other's company in the quiet of your home. I like to call it "full scale lockdown." You've turned off the cell phones, the home phone, the "Crackberry," and the computer. You're not going to let anything from the outside world weasel into your romantic romp. The following recipes are perfect for your low-key movie night. Or whip up a couple of the recipes in my Nibbles chapter to accompany these treats, and you'll have a real feast to kick-start your night.

WHAT'S HOT? · *Candle Wax* · *Fireplaces* · *Cuddling*

Oven Baked Chicken Tenders *with* Honey Mustard Sauce

Here's my healthier, no trans fat version. Soaking the chicken in the brine first adds great flavor.

1 quart of water	3 eggs
2 tablespoons sea salt	1/2 cup milk
1 tablespoon sugar	Salt and pepper to taste
1 teaspoon poultry seasoning	1 cup flour
1 teaspoon garlic powder	2 cups breadcrumbs
1 teaspoon onion powder	6-8 boneless, skinless chicken tenders, rinsed and dried
1 teaspoon Old Bay seasoning	

THE MOVES

1. Make the brine by combining the water, sea salt, sugar, poultry seasoning, garlic powder, onion powder, and the Old Bay seasoning. Make sure everything dissolves in the water.

2. Marinate the chicken tenders in the brine for at least an hour, covered and in the fridge.

3. Preheat oven to 400 degrees F.

4. Combine the eggs, milk, salt, and pepper and mix well.

5. Remove the chicken from the brine and dredge in the flour, shaking off excess.

6. Dunk the chicken into the egg mixture.

7. Dredge the chicken in the breadcrumbs coating both sides evenly.

8. Put the tenders on a nonstick baking sheet and bake for 15 minutes or until golden brown and crunchy.

Serves 2

Honey Mustard Sauce

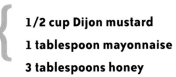

1/2 cup Dijon mustard

1 tablespoon mayonnaise

3 tablespoons honey

THE MOVE

1. Combine all three ingredients in a small bowl and stir until well mixed.

Serves 2

Popcorn Balls

My mom used to make these for me when I was a kid. My favorite movie back then was Grease. *I used to pretend I was Danny Zuko, and I'd dance to "Grease Lightning." All right—too much information...*

{
1 bag microwave popcorn (regular or Kettle Corn flavor)

1 cup honey

2 tablespoons butter

1/2 cup water

2 teaspoon salt

1 teaspoon vanilla extract

Wax paper

THE MOVES

1. Pop the popcorn according to package directions and transfer to a large bowl.

2. In a small saucepan over low heat combine honey, butter, water, salt, and vanilla. Keep the heat low until it starts to boil.

3. Pour the honey mixture slowly over the popcorn.

4. Now it's time to get your hands dirty. Wash your hands in cold water first then start mixing and pressing the popcorn into baseball-size balls.

5. Set popcorn balls on wax paper. Chill in the refrigerator until ready to serve.

Serves 4

✳ 4-1-1 TIPS

* I use Newman's Own popcorn because he gives all the profits to charity.

* If you want to make the balls extra sweet, add a few tablespoons of caramel syrup.

TOP 10 ROMANTIC SONGS

1. **Wonderful Tonight** – *Eric Clapton*
2. **Let's Get It On** – *Marvin Gaye*
3. **Your Body Is A Wonderland** – *John Mayer*
4. **One** – *U2*
5. **In Your Eyes** – *Peter Gabriel*
6. **Let's Go To Bed** – *The Cure*
7. **Crash In To You** – *Dave Matthews Band*
8. **Never Tear Us Apart** – *INXS*
9. **Is This love?** – *Bob Marley*
10. **No Ordinary Love** – *Sade*

TOP 10 DATE MOVIES

1. **The Notebook**
2. **Far and Away**
3. **Say Anything**
4. **When Harry Met Sally**
5. **Ghost**
6. **Shakespeare in Love**
7. **The Blue Lagoon**
8. **While You Were Sleeping**
9. **Garden State**
10. **Pretty Woman**

Social Soirées

DON'T BE A HERMIT—entertaining is how you make new friends and keep your old ones. It's all about timing, themes, and seasons. Don't throw a barbecue party in the middle of winter unless you want to end up out in the freezing cold, by yourself, shivering over the grill while everyone is inside talking and laughing…at you.

Whether it's a double date dinner, a few friends hanging out to watch the big game, or the holidays with family, you'll be covered with these full-proof recipes.

THEME PARTY IDEAS *Birthdays, Cinco de Mayo, Summer Solstice, March Madness, St. Patrick's Day, Cajun Night*

JAMAICAN THEME NIGHT

Any time of the year is appropriate for this popular theme; when it's cold and you wish you were in Jamaica or when it's warm and you still wish you were in Jamaica. I use Blue Mountain Jerk Sauce because it's very tasty and makes this recipe really easy. But just in case you're feeling adventurous, I've included a jerk sauce recipe. The Jamaican Rice and Beans, Baked Bananas and Rum, and Trapped in Paradise recipes all go together to complete this theme party.

This party serves 4-6.

Jamaican Rice and Beans

{
4 boneless, skinless chicken breasts

2 15-ounce cans red kidney beans, drained and rinsed

3 cups uncooked long grain rice

1 green onion, sliced thin

2 cloves garlic, chopped

THE MOVES

1. In a large pot combine beans, rice, green onions, and garlic.

2. Add 6 cups of water.

3. Bring to a boil over high heat. Once boiling, stir and then reduce heat and simmer, covered, for about 20 minutes or until all liquid is absorbed.

4. You can serve this on the plate next to the Jerk Chicken, or you can place the Jerk Chicken on top of a bed of rice.

Trapped in Paradise

This drink will help you pretend you are truly in paradise. This is also great on a hot summer day.

{
1 bottle Malibu Rum

Pineapple juice

Cranberry Juice

Orange Juice

1 lemon

THE MOVES

1. Fill 4 tall glasses halfway with ice and then equal parts of the rum, pineapple juice, cranberry juice, and orange juice.

2. Stir, squeeze a few drops of lemon in each, and enjoy.

Jerk Chicken

For this recipe it's best to marinate the chicken in the sauce for at least 2 hours. This will also give you time to get the Bob Marley music going and get your place organized.

1/2 cup crushed pineapple	1 teaspoon ground cumin
1 teaspoon allspice	1 teaspoon onion powder
1 teaspoon nutmeg	1 teaspoon garlic powder
1/2 cup brown sugar	1 teaspoon cayenne pepper
1 tablespoon soy sauce	4-6 skinless chicken breasts

THE MOVES

1. Combine the pineapple, allspice, nutmeg, sugar, soy sauce, cumin, onion powder, garlic powder, and cayenne pepper in a large bowl. Stir until well combined. Add the chicken and coat well. Cover and put in the fridge to marinate for at least 2 hours, but overnight is best.

2. Preheat oven to 400 degrees F.

3. Transfer chicken to a baking dish and cover.

4. Bake for 30 minutes.

Baked Bananas and Rum

Serve this as dessert for this theme party and you'll really impress your guests.

- **4 ripe bananas, peeled and cut into 1-inch pieces**
- **4 tablespoons brown sugar**
- **1/4 cup rum**
- **1 carton vanilla ice cream**

THE MOVES

1. Preheat oven to 350 degrees F.

2. In a large mixing bowl combine the bananas, brown sugar, and rum. Stir gently to combine.

3. Transfer the banana mixture to a non-stick baking sheet and bake for 20 minutes.

4. Place large scoops of ice cream into separate bowls and pour the baked bananas over the ice cream.

4-1-1 TIPS

* The music for this party should be Bob Marley, Ziggy Marley, or Eek-a-Mouse.
* Serve Red Stripe beer.
* My favorite rum is Mount Gay, but any Jamaican rum will do.

MEXICAN THEME NIGHT

It's *fiesta* time! I recommend serving Dos Equis beer, but I can't recommend any Mexican music, so you'll just have to pull out that sombrero from your last drunken trip to Mexico. Here are some fun recipes to get your fiesta started right. Prepare and serve the appetizers first so as soon as your guests walk in they can get a cold one and a little nibble. *This party serves 4.*

Salsa Fresca

Salsa fresca means fresh salsa. The secret is to add a can of tomato sauce to bind it all together. Making a fresh salsa is always better than eating salsa from a jar because there are no preservatives in the homemade version.

10 tomatoes, chopped

1 bunch cilantro,
stems removed and chopped

1 medium white onion, chopped

5 cayenne peppers, deseeded
and chopped

2 cloves garlic, chopped

1 teaspoon garlic salt

Salt and pepper to taste

1 8-ounce can tomato sauce

THE MOVES

1. In a large bowl combine tomatoes, cilantro, onion, cayenne peppers, garlic, garlic salt, salt, and pepper.

2. Add the tomato sauce and stir, mixing thoroughly.

 4-1-1 TIP
Jalapeños can be substituted for the cayenne peppers.

Roasted Garlic and Parmesan Cheese Guacamole

Being from Los Angeles, where Mexican food is really popular, I've been making this for years. Luckily for us, Haas avocados are available all year long now because they are grown all over the world. Serve this guacamole with blue or white corn tortilla chips.

- **4 Hass avocados, peeled, pit removed, and chopped**
- **3 cloves roasted garlic**
- **Juice of 1/2 lemon**
- **1 teaspoon salt**
- **2 tablespoons Parmesan cheese**

THE MOVES

1. In a large bowl combine avocado, garlic, lemon juice, salt, and cheese.
2. Stir well until creamy.

4-1-1 TIPS

* To make it extra creamy add a bit of sour cream.
* Add a few shakes of hot sauce to give it some spice.

Rosarita Margarita

I discovered these real margaritas while hanging out in Rosarita, Mexico. What's missing is the headache juice, Triple Sec. Instead fresh squeezed lime juice is used.

- **Ice, enough to fill 4 glasses**
- **1 bottle tequila (whichever brand you prefer)**
- **Juice of 16 limes**
- **1 bottle Cointreau**

THE MOVES

1. Fill 4 glasses with ice
2. Add 1 shot tequila, juice of 4 limes, and 1 shot of Cointreau per glass. Mix well.

The Real Deal 6 Layer Dip of Doom

This is always a crowd pleaser, and it's super simple to make and has great flavors. It's also good for a lazy day on the couch—just lean over to the coffee table and dip your chip. Just don't be double dipping!

{
- **1 15-ounce can refried beans**
- **1 cup sour cream**
- **1 cup salsa (use your favorite)**
- **1 cup shredded Mexican cheese blend**
- **1/2 cup chopped jalapeños**
- **1/2 cup sliced black olives**

THE MOVES

1. Spread beans onto bottom of a large pie plate.

2. On top of the beans, first layer the sour cream, then the salsa, cheese, peppers, and olives.

3. Cover and chill in fridge before serving. Serve with blue or red corn tortilla chips.

✳ 4-1-1 TIP

If you would prefer a vegetarian refried bean, Rosarita makes a great one.

Chipotle Chicken and Cheese Enchiladas

This main dish blends three great flavors: chipotle chiles (which are smoked jalapeños), chicken, and cheese. Ask ahead to make sure that all of your guests eat chicken and cheese. If not, make some of the enchiladas with only cheese or only chicken.

4 boneless, skinless chicken breasts

2 tablespoons vegetable oil

1 small onion, diced

1 7-ounce can chipotle chiles in adobo sauce

2 cups shredded pepper Jack cheese

2 tablespoons tomato paste

Salt and pepper to taste

10 corn tortillas, softened

2 cups tomato sauce

THE MOVES

1. Preheat oven to 350 degrees F. Rinse and pat dry the chicken breasts. Place in a baking dish, cover, and cook for 20 minutes or until cooked through. Cool the chicken out of the baking dish and then shred it. Keep the oven hot.

2. In a medium pot over medium heat add the oil and onions and sauté for 5 minutes.

3. Add chicken, chiles, 1/2 of the cheese, tomato paste, salt, and pepper. Stir until blended. Take off the heat and set aside.

4. Warm the tortillas by placing them in the oven for 1 minute. When warmed, fill each tortilla evenly with the chicken mixture and roll into an enchilada. Continue until all the tortillas have been used, transferring each enchilada to the baking dish as you complete it.

5. Pour tomato sauce over the enchiladas. Cover with the remaining cheese.

6. Bake for 20 minutes or until cheese is bubbling.

HAWAIIAN NIGHT

I haven't been to Hawaii in so long I have to pretend to escape there. The second I take a sip of my homemade Mai Tai, I can hear the ocean waves breaking and feel the clean air blowing in my face. If you and your friends are over worked and underpaid and can't get away for more than a night, then try some of these vacation quenching recipes to help alleviate the pain of the everyday grind.

The perfect music for this theme party is the CD *Somewhere over the Rainbow* by Israel Kamakawiwo'ole. And don't forget to get "leid."

This party serves 4.

Maui Spareribs

When I was in Maui I created these tasty morsels by fooling around with all the different fresh fruits and juices available there. All I can say is get the wet-naps out. Shaka bra!

{
1 cup pineapple juice

1/2 cup honey mustard

1 cup guava juice

5 cloves garlic, minced

1 tablespoon grated fresh ginger

5 pounds baby back ribs, individually cut

THE MOVES

1. In a large bowl combine the pineapple juice, honey mustard, guava juice, garlic, and ginger. Add the ribs, cover, and marinate in the fridge for at least an hour.

2. Preheat the oven to 350 degrees F and bake for about 45 minutes or until the ribs are barely pink near the bone.

Kalua Pig

Kalua means "the pit" in Hawaiian. Don't worry; you don't have to dig a big hole in your backyard. However this is the perfect recipe for pulling out that Crock-pot you got from Nana for Christmas. Cooking pork is all about slow and low, and what is slower cooking than with a Crock-pot?

{
1 3-5 pound pork loin, excess fat removed

3 tablespoons sea salt

1 tablespoon liquid smoke

1/2 cup apple juice

1/2 cup pineapple juice

THE MOVES

1. Pierce the pork all over with a knife. Rub the salt over the pork, and then rub with the liquid smoke.

2. Turn the Crock-pot to low and add the juice and the pork. Cover and cook for 10 hours, turning halfway.

3. Remove the cooked pork from the Crock-pot, place it on large plate, and shred the meat using 2 forks. Serve with macaroni salad.

Macaroni Salad

This is the traditional macaroni salad I had at a local hangout in Hawaii.

{
1 pound large macaroni noodles

1/4 cup grated carrots

1 cup mayonnaise

1/4 cup milk

Salt and pepper to taste

THE MOVES

1. Cook macaroni in a medium pot according to package directions. Drain, transfer to a large bowl, and cool.

2. Add carrots, mayonnaise, milk, salt, and pepper. Stir until well mixed.

3. Cover and chill in the fridge until ready to serve.

Mai Tai

So here's the story with Mai Tais. At first Trader Vic claimed he was the inventor of the so-sexy drink. But actually it was Don the Beachcomber who actually invented the Mai Tai. Here are their two versions of the Mai Tai and the super tasty recipe I created the last time I was in Hawaii.

Don the Beachcomber's Original Mai Tai

1 1/2 ounces Myers Plantation rum

1 ounce Cuban rum

3/4 ounce lime juice

1 ounce grapefruit juice

1/4 ounce falernum

1/2 ounce Cointreau

2 dashes angostura bitters

1 dash Pernod

Rind of 1 squeezed lime

1 cup cracked ice

4 springs of mint

1 pineapple spear

THE MOVES

1. Combine first 10 ingredients in a blender and blend for 1 minute on medium speed.

2. Garnish with 4 sprigs of mint and a spear of pineapple.

 4-1-1 TIP

Don't think you can cheat and use the sweet and sour mix. That's a filler and it won't taste the same.

Trader Vic's Original Mai Tai

{
2 ounces 17-year-old J. Wray Nephew rum

1/2 ounce French garnier orgeat

1/2 ounce, Holland DeKuyper orange curaçao

1/4 ounce rock candy syrup

Juice of 1 lime

1 lime wedge

1 sprig fresh mint

THE MOVES

1. In a cocktail shaker combine the first 5 ingredients and shake until mixed. Pour into a glass and garnish with a lime wedge and a sprig of fresh mint.

My Super Tasty Mai Tai

I don't know why this super tasty recipe became so complicated. I suppose it was when I wouldn't pay $10.00 for a Mai Tai at the bar. After a quick trip to the store I created probably the best Mai Tai ever.

{
Ice to fill a large cup

2 ounces light rum

2 ounces pineapple juice

2 ounces guava juice

2 ounces orange juice

1 ounce Trader Vic's Mai Tai mix

1 ounce Myers dark run

THE MOVE

1. In a large cup combine ice, light rum, pineapple juice, guava juice, orange juice, Mai Tai mix, and dark rum. Stir until mixed.

APHRODISIAC #17: Dark Chocolate

The Aztecs referred to chocolate as "nourishment of the gods." Chocolate contains chemicals thought to effect neurotransmitters in the brain. Dark chocolate contains more antioxidants than blueberries and red wine. If you want a double whammy of love, try dark chocolate and red wine together.

APHRODISIAC #18:
Pineapples, Mangoes, Papayas

Used in the homeopathic treatment for impotence, these three fruits have an adventurous, romantic flare to them.

APHRODISIAC #19: Ginger

This root is the ancient Chinese secret for longevity and virility. Ginger root raw, cooked, or crystallized is a stimulant to the circulatory system and boosts the immune system. It also gives that warm and fuzzy feeling that creates the perfect atmosphere for cuddling.

APHRODISIAC #20:
Kissing on the neck and massages...

Touch and intimacy are the keys to romance. Light and sensual kisses and body massages will always do the trick with your loved one.

There's no recipe for this either. You either got or you don't.

Liquid Love

IT'S SO EXPENSIVE TO go out and have drinks, and when you do go to a bar the music is cranking so loudly you have to yell at your date the entire night. Then you wake up with no voice, no love, and a receipt totaling $68.00. So why not stay home and with a little effort save your voice, your bank account, and actually have a conversation. I call that the trifecta of love.

We all have our favorite cocktails and rarely deviate from them when we're out at a bar or restaurant. I promise you'll be turned on to a new drink from this section. All of these drinks are fun to make for guests or a date. There are three sections, one for cold drinks, one for hot drinks (a.k.a Hot Toddies), and one for the top 5 guy and gal drinks.

WHAT'S HOT? • *Anything pomegranate* • *Mojitos* • *Dirty martinis*

Homemade Wine Coolers

When it's a beautiful day and you just want to kick it at the pool, on the patio, or in the backyard, drink this refreshing cocktail. My friends call this my "Man Spritzer," even though I don't like that name too much.

1 tray of ice cubes

1 bottle Chardonnay

1 lemon, cut into wedge quarters

1 orange, cut into wedge quarters

1 16-ounce bottle of lemon-lime soda

THE MOVES

1. Fill 4 wine glasses with ice.
2. Fill each glass halfway with wine.
3. Squeeze 1 lemon wedge into each glass.
4. Squeeze 1 orange wedge into each glass.
5. Fill the glasses the rest of the way with the lemon-lime soda.
6. Stir and serve.

Serves 4

Jones Vodka Slushy

Jones soda has some great flavors, and it's all natural. Pick the flavor you like best for this drink.

{
2 cups cubed ice

1 12-ounce bottle Jones flavored soda

4 shots vodka

THE MOVES

1. In a blender combine ice, Jones soda, and vodka.
2. Blend until nice and slushy.
3. Pour into two glasses.

Serves 2

Blood Orange Screwdriver

Blood oranges are the best of the orange family. Unfortunately, they only come into season once a year. As soon as you see them, make this original screwdriver.

{
Cubed ice

4 shots vodka

Juice of 10 blood oranges

THE MOVES

1. Fill two glasses with ice.
2. Add 2 shots of vodka per glass.
3. Divide orange juice equally and add to each glass. Stir.

Serves 2

Guinness and Cider

For some reason Guinness and apple cider go great together. Woodchuck cider is the best, but it's hard to find. Hornsby's is also very good. If you want to make your own version of these hard ciders, here's a simple recipe.

{
1 12-ounce can or bottle Guinness

1 12-ounce bottle apple cider

THE MOVES

1. Fill two beer glasses halfway with Guinness and halfway with cider. Stir.

Serves 2

Sexy Sangria

This is what I bring to all the get-togethers and parties I go to. Friends call me before and ask if I'm bringing the "secret sauce." The last time I made this everyone got naked and jumped in the pool. I'm just glad it was heated. You need a big container for this one.

4 bottles (750 ml) red wine

1 cup sugar

5 oranges

2 lemons

2 limes

1 green apple, cored and sliced thin

2 cups brandy

THE MOVES

1. In a large pitcher combine the red wine and sugar and stir until sugar is dissolved.
2. Cut the oranges, lemons, and limes in half and squeeze their juice directly into the pitcher.
3. Add the green apple pieces.
4. Add the brandy and stir. Cover and chill for as long as possible before serving. Serve with or without ice.

Serves 4-8

White Sangria with Lychee Fruit

This recipe is inspired by this really cool place called Republic in New York's Union Square. Pronounced lie-chee, this Asian fruit is so flavorful it makes this sangria unique.

1 bottle white wine

1 cup brandy

1 cup passion fruit juice

1 apple, diced

1 pear, diced

1 orange, peeled and cut in bite-size pieces

1 15-ounce can lychee

THE MOVES

1. In a large pitcher combine wine, brandy, fruit juice, apple, pear, orange, and the can of lychee including the juice. Stir until well mixed.
2. Cover and chill until ready to serve. Serve with or without ice.

Serves 2

Bloody Mary of Doom

I can't tell you how many times I have had these with a great breakfast on a Saturday or Sunday morning with a girlfriend. There's something about a good Bloody Mary that gets everyone fired up.

{
Crushed ice

2 shots vodka

1 teaspoon Worcestershire sauce

1/2 teaspoon celery salt

Dash of A-1 steak sauce

Dash of hot sauce

1/2 teaspoon prepared horseradish

Pepper to taste

1/2 cup tomato juice

THE MOVES

1. Fill each glass halfway with ice.
2. Add vodka, Worcestershire, celery salt, steak sauce, hot sauce, horseradish, and pepper.
3. Fill rest of glass up with tomato juice and stir.

Serves 2

Dirty Russian

My friend, Marc Merrie, makes this tequila-inspired recipe. He recommends using Cazadores Reposado tequila, but any white tequila will do. Also, Negra Modelo Mexican beer is recommended, but if all you have is Tecate, that's fine.

{
1/4 cup salt

Cubed or crushed ice

Juice of 1 lime

4 dashes hot sauce

4 dashes Worcestershire sauce

2 shots tequila

2 bottles Negra Modelo Beer

THE MOVES

1. Wet the rim of each glass. Pour the salt onto a plate and place the glasses rim down into the salt to get a nice ring of salt on the rim. Fill each glass halfway with ice.
2. Divide the lime juice equally and add to each glass.
3. Add the hot sauce, the Worcestershire sauce, and tequila equally to each glass.
4. Fill the rest of the glasses up with the beer and stir.

Serves 2

HOT TODDY

Any mixed drink that is served hot is called a hot toddy. Although it originated in Scotland, there are many variations. The essential ingredients are as follows: A spirit of some sort, such as brandy, rum, or whiskey. A hot liquid of some sort, such as tea, coffee, cocoa, or water. A sweetener of some sort, such as honey, sugar, or syrup. Sometimes spices are added, such as cinnamon or cloves. Sometimes a citrus juice is added, such as lemon or orange.

The following hot toddy recipes are great when your soul is cold and needs a little warming up. Hot toddies (such as mulled cider) are typically enjoyed while chilling out in the evening or after being outside on a cold day.

Basic Hot Toddy

{
2 ounces whiskey

2 ounces honey

2 ounces lemon juice

6 ounces hot water

THE MOVE
1. Combine all ingredients, stir, and divide between two mugs.

Serves 2

The Radiator

{
1/2 cup hot chocolate

4 ounces Dr. McGillicuddy's peppermint schnapps

1/2 cup coffee
}

THE MOVES
1. Combine all ingredients, stir, and divide between two large coffee mugs.

Serves 2

Healthy Ginger Drink

When you feel run down and like you're about to get sick, or if you are sick, this drink will kick your immune system right back into gear. Ginger is truly the "Ancient Chinese Secret."

{
24 ounces water   **5 lemons or limes**

2 tablespoons sliced ginger root   **1/2 cup honey**
}

THE MOVES
1. Bring the water to a boil.
2. Add ginger and boil over medium heat for 15-20 minutes.
3. Cut the lemons or limes in half. Squeeze the lemon or lime juice right into pot and then add the rind from one lemon.
4. Add the honey and remove from heat.
5. Stir well before pouring into a mug.

Serves 4

Hot Soy

Try this comfort drink on those cold nights when you are relaxing. Not everything has to have alcohol in it, but a shot of brandy added to this will help you sleep like a baby. Sweet dreams!

{
2 cups soy milk   Optional:

2 tea bags of your favorite herbal tea,   **2 shots brandy or cognac**
such as chamomile
}

THE MOVES
1. Heat up the milk in the microwave or in a saucepan over the stove.
2. Once the milk is steaming, add the teabag and seep for 3-5 minutes.
3. Divide equally into two mugs. Add brandy or cognac.

Serves 2

Top 5 Guy Drinks

#1 Vodka Cranberry
4 ounces vodka • 10 ounces cranberry juice • Juice of 2 limes
Combine all ingredients, stir, and divide equally in two glasses over ice.
Serves 2

#2 The Manhattan
1 ounce sweet vermouth • 4 ounces blended whiskey • 2 dash angostura bitters
Combine all ingredients, stir, and divide equally in two glasses over ice.
Serves 2

#3 Tequila Sunrise
1 ounce grenadine • 6 ounces orange juice • 4 ounces tequila • Juice of 1 lime
Combine all ingredients, stir, and divide equally in two glasses over ice.
Serves 2

#4 Orgasm
1 ounce Irish cream • 1 ounce peppermint schnapps
Divide ingredients equally between two shot glasses, and drink!
Serves 2

Vodka Red Bull
The last time I drank a few of these, I danced all night—and I don't even dance!
4 ounces vodka • 2 cans Red Bull
Combine all ingredients, stir, and divide equally in two glasses over ice.
Serves 2

Top 5 Gal Drinks

#1 Pomegranate Martini
4 ounces citrus vodka • Juice of 1 lemon • 1/2 ounce pomegranate juice • 2 ounces simple syrup or Cointreau
Shake all ingredients well with ice and strain into two chilled martini glasses.
Serves 2

#2 Mojito
Crushed ice • Juice of 1 lime • 2 teaspoons sugar • 10 sprigs mint • Crushed ice • 3 ounces light rum • Schweppes club soda
Fill two glasses with crushed ice. In a separate glass combine lime juice, sugar, and 8 sprigs of mint. Stir until sugar is dissolved and mint becomes fragrant and then divide equally into the glasses with the ice. Add rum and then fill the rest of the glasses with club soda. Garnish with remaining mint sprigs.
Serves 2

#3 Sex on the Beach
6 ounces cranberry juice • 6 ounces orange or pineapple juice • 2 ounces peach schnapps • 2 ounces vodka
Combine all ingredients, stir, and divide equally in two glasses over ice.
Serves 1

#4 Appletini
4 ounces vodka • 2 ounces apple liqueur • Ice • 2 thin slice of apple
Combine vodka and apple liqueur in a cocktail mixer with plenty of ice, shake, and strain into two chilled martini glasses. Garnish with a thin wedge of sliced apple.
Serves 2

#5 New School Cosmo
Ice • 1 ounce Cointreau or Triple Sec • 1 ounce cranberry juice • 1 ounce orange juice • 3 ounces vodka • 2 dashes lime juice • 2 lime wedges
Combine all the ingredients except the lime wedge in a cocktail mixer with plenty of ice, shake, and strain into two chilled cocktail glasses. Garnish with the lime wedge.
Serves 2

Acknowledgements

I WANT TO KISS YOU and thank you for your support, inspiration, and recipes.

To my family: Mom—Ella Roberts; Nana—Opal Roberts; Aunt Janice, Uncle Richard, and all my relatives now scattered all over the country. Thanks for all of your unconditional love and support throughout the years.

To my Northland Publishing crew: Thanks for the opportunity to do this book. I will stay on the road until I look like Yoda to make this book successful. Claudine Randazzo, Sunny Yang, Brian Billideau, Dave Jenney, Eric Howard, Linda Kranz, David Romine, and Dave Alston. And of course, I can't forget the photographer who made the book look great, Christopher Marchetti.

To my agent: Deborah Obad—We make a great team! Hey, where's my TV show?!

To my PR Crew: Stacey Bender, Rob Hammerling—where's my check? Lisa Miller Jagniatkowski, Victor Domine, Patty Murphy, and the rest of the ladies working their tales off to make The Food Dude Empire live long.

To my Lordly & Dame college tour crew: Thanks for all of your help while I travel across this great land of ours horrifying college students by the hundreds. Kevin MacCrae, Karen Howley, David LaCamera, and Jessica Starr-Glick. And of course, Debbie MacCrae and the kids: Chris, Mark, and Sean. Thanks for putting up with me & letting me sleep in the spare bedroom with the heat off even though it was freezing in Boston.

I can't forget Bob Bernarduci, Mike and Jenny Ciampa, Dan Hurd, Rich Synnott, Brittany Donnelly, Peter Schwartz, Jim Daniels, Colin & Sarah MacKay, and Bonnie Shannon.

A special thanks to all of the chefs whose great senses of taste and flavor inspired me to make my own recipes: Lourdes Montes Kirby, Sheila Montes Kirby, and the Mayor of the East Village Chad Cavanaugh: I'm in Philipino Heaven! Rodney Wedge and Connie Chatham at Fuego! Atlanta: Cal Evans: You make a mean breakfast. Marc Marrie: You make a mean cocktail. Deborah MacRae: Can't wait to have more of that hot soup. Thanks Aunt Val for the Spicy Spaghetti Sauce; may you rest in peace. Thanks Mom for feeding me the Light Lasagna all these years. Green Beans and Mushrooms inspired by Fish Market in San Diego, CA. Maryland Lump Crab Cakes inspired by Brian Malarkey, Mike Mitchell & The Oceanaire Seafood Room. White Sangria inspired by Republic restaurant in Union Square, N.Y. Thad Roenitz: Keep warm drinking the hot toddies at Lambeau Field.

Index